Living the Dream
with
Andy Payton

Gavin Roper

Published by Bruce Publishing 2011 (First Edition)

All of the enclosed contents are the experiences and explanations directly from Andrew Payton. None of the enclosed material has been used without authority from Andrew Payton which is believed to be true. The enclosed material has been confirmed from Andrew Payton during interviews. Andrew Payton has agreed for all the enclosed to be printed of which he has confirmed took place. No other party other than Andrew Payton has had any other influence of the contents in writing this book.

ISBN: 978-0-9563353-7-1

Acknowledgements

Gavin Roper (Mr. Nice Guy: dedication and loyal MUST be his middle names). Gavin has sat with me for the last 12 months, coming down to my house at all hours to work on this project. Without Gavin, this book would never have happened; he's a very patient, walking business directory.

Carol Love (no fingers left), the master of all keyboards; she has worked tirelessly for hours on end typing up the book from Gavin's Dictaphone. How did she ever understand my strong Burnley accent?!

Tony Dawber has edited this book. Tony Dawber, editor and publisher of the UK edition of the Brian Jensen book *Beast*; Dave Burnley's best-selling autobiography *Got To Be There*; *God is a DJ - But He Only Warms Up For Sasha*, a biography of the superstar DJ; and a number of other sports and general publications.

Wayne Miller, who managed to get me into the professional game.

Burnley Express - especially **Chris Boden**, for giving me the positive publicity and supplying some excellent photos for the book.

My Mum/Dad (Carol and Dave), along with my three daughters (Olivia, Georgia and Lauren), brother (David) and sister (Lyndsey), who have all enjoyed my rollercoaster career.

The fans that have supported me through good and bad times.

Contents

The nightmare that I never wanted

Let's get one thing straight. I'm a lifelong Burnley fan.

It was always my dream to play for them, and therefore, when I was released by my beloved Clarets as a kid, I was devastated.

So, imagine my feelings the day I finally got to play on the sacred ground of Turf Moor – but not as a Claret.

Instead, I was in the colours of opponents Barnsley, and, sure enough, I silenced the very fans I used to stand with on the terraces by grabbing the winning goal.

But I didn't celebrate as a player normally would, and if you understand my feelings and emotions on that day, you'd know why.

Put it this way, I'd played in the Old Firm clash in Glasgow before I came to Turf Moor that day with Barnsley, and I felt more nervous than I did when I played for Celtic against Rangers in front of 60,000, and that's a fact.

I can recall vividly the day I was released by Burnley. When I was told, I was basically devastated, absolutely devastated. I was 16 years old at the time, Burnley born and bred, and went to every home game.

I had signed schoolboy forms with the Clarets and I had turned down Hull after I had also signed schoolboy forms for them when I was 13.

Burnley took on 10 lads that year on the old YTS scheme, which was free for them as all costs were paid by the Government. If I had been taken on, I could have lived at home with my parents and it would have been great.

So when I was knocked back, it was a double whammy, really. Not only were they saying to me that they did not think I was good enough, but, as I said, the scheme was free for them and they still didn't want me. That made it worse and I can't describe how devastated I was.

Ashley Hoskin, who is still on the coaching staff, was taken on that year, but he was the only one of that intake that made it. All the others got released. Hoskin is the stand out one because he actually broke into the first team at Burnley when he was quite young.

They had a final trial down at Gawthorpe training ground and my dad went down to watch me. They had schoolboys from all over England, Wales, Scotland and Ireland, as Burnley had a big scouting network. I actually got a hat trick and we won 5-3, but I still didn't get taken on.

They said to my dad: "We can't say yes and we can't say no." Then they kept me waiting for three weeks and then I was told by Arthur Bellamy. He has since said he made a mistake, so fair play to him; but I was absolutely devastated.

I still felt I should definitely have been taken on. The only thing that really kept me going when I went to Hull was the belief that I should have been taken on by Burnley and that I was good enough.

Obviously, I'd gone to Hull, then I was Middlesbrough's

record signing, and then I went up to Celtic for a couple of years before I ended up at Barnsley.

When I was at Hull, Burnley were always in the lower divisions, while we were in what is now the Championship; but I always looked out for their results, because I was a Clarets fan.

Yet I never actually thought I would play against them until Burnley got promoted in 1993/94 while I was at Barnsley and the fixtures came out. I saw we were playing at Turf Moor in September and I thought: "Here we go."

By then I had already had a season at Barnsley and scored a lot of goals. I had been top scorer and established myself in the team and Barnsley had a good side; but I must admit I wasn't relishing the thought of coming to Turf Moor, because I was going to have to play against a team I supported.

The season had just got under way and we'd played about half a dozen games and had a decent start, and Burnley had not had a bad start as well. I was in the side and was fit, so I knew I'd play, and that was confirmed 48 hours before the game, as was the norm at the club.

The night before the game I was unbelievably nervous. The situation didn't mean much to the Barnsley people, but I still lived in Burnley and I'd also made it clear that I was a Burnley fan and I'd never played at Turf Moor, not even as a kid, and clearly I knew a lot of people in the town, so everyone knew it was a big deal for me.

We normally stayed over before an away game and this was no different, so I found myself at the Oaks Hotel with the Barnsley team.

It's amazing to think that even though it wasn't that long ago, mobile phones weren't around, so there were no people texting me, as there would be today. But everybody knew I was playing for Barnsley at Turf Moor that day, and it was such a big game for me that it was no surprise I was nervous and apprehensive.

There was a big crowd, upwards of 15,000, with a good Barnsley following, but it was a surreal atmosphere because the moment I walked onto the pitch was the moment when I knew how much I wanted to play for Burnley - even more than I'd previously thought.

I'd made my mind up that if I did score I wasn't going to celebrate; but obviously a lot of people probably expected me to do the opposite, as I would have shown I'd proved the club wrong in rejecting me.

Turf Moor hadn't changed from when I was a lad, but obviously on this day I was seeing it from the players' angle. I used to walk around the ground and go and stand on the Beehole End, but this time the coach pulled up outside the entrance to the dressing rooms, which was all new to me.

I felt as though I was on a bit of a hiding to nothing because I thought, if I get murdered, people will say, "Well, he wasn't good enough anyway"; and if I did well, the same people might not be happy because I wasn't doing it for Burnley.

I was really nervous and apprehensive and when you get into that mode you just want to get it over with and get a result.

One of the first people I saw when I arrived was John Mullin, who I already knew and I actually ended up playing with for Burnley at a later date. John had not got in the squad that day and, as I was walking up the tunnel, he was walking down. He said: "All the best, Payts." Perhaps that was because he wasn't playing and maybe he wanted us to win. That's how it sometimes works.

I walked on to the pitch, having a look round at all the Burnley fans, and then, as I went back to the dressing room, I noticed Barnsley had a couple of thousand in the old away section of the Longside, and it looked like a good atmosphere building up.

Jimmy Mullen was Burnley manager at the time, while we had a player/manager in Danny Wilson, who was actually playing that day.

We also had ex-Claret Brendan O'Connell and the likes of Gerry Taggart, Neil Redfearn, Owen Archdeacon, Darren Sheridan, Andy Liddell and Andy Rammell; so with all those guys it was clear we had a good side.

I knew quite a lot of the Burnley players. I was with Gary Parkinson at Middlesbrough, so I knew him well. It's really sad that he's had such a bad illness recently. I also knew the likes of David Eyres, John Deary and John Francis, and they all knew of my Burnley connections, as I think most people in the ground did.

How did it go? Well, sure enough, Barnsley won 1-0 and I scored the winner.

The game was fairly even to begin with and both teams had their chances, but then came the goal which I can remember very clearly.

We got a free kick on the edge of the right-hand side of

the box, and Danny Wilson put the ball in. I feinted to make a near-post run, but pulled off and Gary Parkinson, who was marking me, carried on going, so I just stepped back and had a free header from the edge of the six-yard box. Marlon Beresford was in goal, but he had no chance and I just buried it in the bottom corner.

When the ball went in, obviously as a striker I was glad I scored, especially as it was so early in the game. It all went very quiet, apart from the Barnsley end, which was going mad, of course.

But then a funny feeling came over me.

Normally you would run over to your own fans and celebrate with your team-mates, but, though Brendan O'Connell and Danny were trying to get me to at least smile, I decided just to walk back.

I felt then I was somehow fated to play for Burnley in the future, and when I think about it now I guess I must be the only person to have scored at Turf Moor and not celebrated their goal. I've been on the ground hundreds of times as a player and fan and I've never seen any other away player not celebrate scoring. I genuinely didn't even smile; I just walked back to the half-way line with this very weird feeling.

Part of me was glad, because obviously I'd proved them wrong; but then again I'd already done that because I'd already scored more than 100 goals for other clubs. It was just that, as a life-long fan, it genuinely hurt scoring against Burnley.

I believe the Burnley fans actually respected the fact that I didn't run round celebrating, because I think it would have caused offence. I've seen other players go back to their old clubs and score and go absolutely berserk, but I didn't want to do that, and my feeling about fate was proved right as, of course, I ended up as a player at Turf Moor.

When the final whistle went, I felt inside that I was glad I'd scored a goal because it showed everybody at Burnley what they were missing, and I can't deny the fact that part of me was pleased because I'd sort of got my own back.

But there was definitely a part of me that was down about it, which is weird in a way.

And what people remember less is that I also scored in the reverse fixture at Barnsley later in the season when we won 2-0, and I did exactly the same thing again. I didn't celebrate at all.

I'm absolutely certain that even the Burnley fans who didn't know me respected that, and it helped when I actually played for them, because I always had a brilliant relationship with the Burnley fans. Maybe it's because I'm one, too.

Chapter 1 My Claret Dream

I had grown up living at home with my mum and dad and my brother David, who is 18 months older than me, in Kings Drive, Hapton. I went to Padiham St John's Primary School and basically started kicking a ball about, I think, probably at the age of about five or six.

I remember getting into the school team when I was a first-year at Padiham St John's, aged about seven, and I remember we actually had a lad called David Byran, who I think went on to play for England Schoolboys at Wembley.

David was four years older than me and he was captain of St John's, and he picked me for the team for a game against Padiham County Primary School. I was sub and I must have been about two feet in height, but I got on and kicked the ball a few times, so I obviously just got the bug then and it was just a case of playing football morning, noon and night from then on. There used to be about 20 lads playing every night on the fields near us.

My older brother David played football, but not at a great level, though he watched nearly every game I played and continued to do so at all the clubs I eventually played at all over England and Scotland, even reserve games. David ended up becoming a big factor in my life with his support and obviously deserves a lot of thanks for that.

My dad, however, never kicked a ball in his life. He was a carpet fitter and just was not into football, though he watched me play for Burnley and other clubs throughout my career.

My mum worked in an office and also had no interest in football, and though my uncle played for a pub team, there was no real family connection with the game, though my dad once said my late grandmother's uncle, whose surname was Dawson, once played for Accrington Stanley years and years ago.

At Padiham St John's, we won the local seven-a-side competition, the Hartley Cup, two years running and I had started scoring a lot of goals; so, at the age of nine, I joined a club called Highfield after my dad saw an advert in the local paper asking for junior players. A guy called Wayne Miller was the manager and was the one who ended up getting me a trial at Hull. We had a really good team, all local lads, and we won everything.

I have always hated the thought of being big-headed, but at St John's I was probably the best player in the team, even though I was playing in the team for lads the year above my own year. And, at the age of 10, I was picked for the Burnley town team, which proves I was doing well.

I remember scoring loads of goals for them, even though I was playing on the right wing at the time because I was really small. My mum claims that even when I signed for Hull, I was still only about five feet one.

One game I particularly recall was when we won 10-0,

and I scored five and the other five were scored by current Burnley star Jay Rodriguez's dad, Kiko.

I was a regular in the town team and I was also training on Tuesday nights at Turf Moor with the Junior Clarets team, who passed on to the club any youngsters showing promise.

Wayne Miller used to write away to clubs asking for trials for the lads at Highfield, and he got me that trial at Hull City. They were near the bottom of the old Fourth Division at the time, but I went over for a trial for a week and I really enjoyed it. I was 13 years old and in digs with these lads and training every day at the club, so it was really different and I thought it was great.

Then Hull asked me to sign schoolboy forms, but Burnley also asked me at the same time and obviously, being a Burnley fan, I opted to sign for the Clarets.

Hull always said, "If it doesn't work out, get back in touch with us", and obviously, as things worked out, I'm glad they did. A lot of thanks definitely go to Wayne Miller, who sorted out that trial for me and actually took me over there and picked me up, because I was only about 13 at the time.

After I signed schoolboy forms for Burnley, I went training every week and was doing OK, or so I thought, scoring goals in A team games and generally doing well. But then there was a change in the management at Burnley. John Bond came in and brought a load of new staff with him, and they were bringing lads in from here, there and everywhere, and just totally overlooking the local lads.

There was a final trial and I scored a hat-trick, which you might imagine would clinch an offer; but then they took all the parents back to Turf Moor and said to my dad: "Well, we can't say yes and we can't say no." To cut a long story short, they kept me hanging on for about three weeks before they finally released me.

What really hurt was that the YTS scheme was free, so it would not have cost them a penny to keep me on, but they didn't. I guess it must just have been fate.

I didn't know what to do, so I got in touch with Wayne Miller, who got back in touch with Hull for me. They remembered me and offered me a week's trial, so I had to go over there for a week, knowing that it was either a YTS at Hull or being a carpenter for my dad; but luckily I did well in the week and they offered me a place on their YTS programme.

So, at 16 years old, I had to leave for Hull, which was a five-hour bus journey, unless I got a lift in my dad's car. Leaving home at that age is tough because at 16 you think you are a man at the time, but you're not, you're a kid.

I lived with an old lady in Hull. Rose Oliver was her name; she was a nice old woman who looked after me well, but there were 10 of us on the YTS and all the other nine were from Hull, and they made my life a misery to begin with. I settled in a bit eventually, but it was really, really hard work, because we all knew we had one year and then we were either going to be taken on or released, so it was unbelievably dog-eat-dog.

I was classed as the outsider big time. They absolutely slaughtered my accent and apprentices can be as cruel as school kids. They hid my kit and things and generally made it really hard. To be honest, I nearly quit a few times in the first three months, because it was hard work, getting all the crap jobs and being treated like an outsider. They were jealous in case I got on and they didn't, and it was worse because they all knew each other and I didn't know anyone.

They had a habit of every day hiding the packed lunch my landlady put me up. I started hiding it myself so they wouldn't nick it, but it still went missing every single day. On this particular day, we had been sweeping the terraces, which wasn't unusual as we were like dogsbodies at Hull. I ran back to my place in the dressing room and there was an apple there, so I grabbed hold of it and started eating it. But every single one of them had wiped their arses and, to put it bluntly, their bell end on it. I didn't realise till I took a bite out of it and they all started laughing and I nearly gagged. They could be so cruel.

Some of the others did make it too, though. Dean Windass was one and there were some good players in the Hull youth team at the time, such as Lee Jenkinson, who went to Coventry for half a million; Mike Smith, who became a regular in Hull's first team and went to Ayr United; Les Thompson, who ended up at Burnley; Nicky Brown and Neil Buckley; all of whom played in the first team at Hull. I reckon seven of that youth team got into the first team eventually, which was a really good success rate.

I did manage to make a few friends when I became a regular in the youth team and was good mates with Mike Smith, once I got established in that team. It helped because the league we were playing in, the Northern Intermediate

League, was a really tough competition, as we played the likes of Newcastle, Leeds and Sheffield United, and once the other lads knew I was up for getting stuck in, they accepted me more, though even that took about four months and they still took the mickey out of my accent. It was "A'r reet, Andy" every single morning, and even the coaches used to do it. It was hard work.

I remember one incident when I got into the reserves and we had an away game. They used to give us £1 to spend at the services, but as we had two games in two days, the coach, Dennis Booth, who was Brian Horton's assistant, said: "Right, now you get your quids." I said in front of everyone: "What? Are we getting £2? How's it going to work, this?" Dennis tried to explain it, but everyone just all started pissing themselves laughing, and all I got every day for the next three weeks was "£1 per person per day?".

Hull only kept on two of the 10 first-year YTS apprentices, so you were always on pins and every time you had a bad game; you were thinking you were going to be released ... but that's the system and you had to accept it.

I was lucky enough to be kept on and went onto what they called a 'young worker's scheme', which gave you a rise of about a fiver a week, and then when I turned 18 I signed as a full-time professional.

I was on £70 a week when I signed as a pro, but I was taking home £58 and had to pay £30 a week for digs, so I was actually £7 a week worse off than when I was an apprentice. That might not sound that much these days, but it did then because we were on absolute utter peanuts. I look at how much kids earn now in football and it amazes me to think I broke into Hull's first team at the level of what is now the Championship and scored on my debut, all while I was on £58 a week take-home pay.

But I have to say that Brian Horton was a big influence on me and an absolutely brilliant manager. He was a real disciplinarian who had us all absolutely on pins, but he was a superb coach as well and he always knew if you weren't putting it in.

I have so much respect for him and his assistant, Dennis Booth, who had coached all over the place, including a spell at Aston Villa. He was a superb coach. Playing under those two was great for me and the best thing that could have happened to me was going to Hull at that time.

I was there three years before I eventually got into the first team at the age of 19. You started off as a junior, and then if you were good enough and you were kept on you got into the reserves when you were about 17.

The reserve league was brilliant in those days, whether it was our league or the Central League: then you played Liverpool at Anfield or Man United at Old Trafford and there would always be some first teamers in there, so it was a really tough league.

Before I actually got into the first team, I'd scored 25 goals for the reserves and really worked my way up. Hull was a massive part of my life at that time. I won the young player of the year award a couple of times and I was also reserve team player of the year, but then I went off to New Zealand.

That move came about because a guy from Hull called

Don Fenton, who'd emigrated to New Zealand in 1958 and was doing some coaching there, asked Hull City if they could take a reserve team striker for three months during our close season.

The season had finished and I was just ready to come home to Burnley and was looking forward to a break when Brian Horton pulled me over to one side and told me I was going to New Zealand. He didn't ask me, he just told me, but I thought it would be a great experience for a 19-year-old to play on the other side of the world and it proved to be fantastic.

I played for three months and did really well, scoring 15 goals in 12 games for a team called PVU Polerview United, who were based just outside Wellington. I didn't score in my first two games, but then I went goal crazy. We won one game 4-0 and I got all four and the whole experience just filled me with confidence for when I came home, which was very important, because scoring is all about confidence.

The standard and facilities were probably on a par with the semi-professional level at home. There were no massive stands or anything like that, but the crowds were reasonable.

It was tough because I was still only 19 and up against older, more experienced players, and if you were an import there was more pressure; but I did well and just the fact that you were on your own on the other side of the world at that age heightened the experience and I really enjoyed it.

Don Fenton's son played in the team and I actually stayed at his house with his wife, daughter and son, and he must have let Hull know I was doing OK; but that counted for nothing when I got back to the UK. But, thankfully, I was raring to go when I got back and hit the ground running, and that's when I broke into the first team.

The future England manager, Steve McClaren, was in the team at the time, as was big Billy Whitehurst, who eventually went to Newcastle in a £250,000 deal. Brian Horton was still turning out and was player/manager and we also had Gareth Roberts, who was a great club servant.

But perhaps the most influential for me was Keith Edwards, who in reality taught me my trade. Keith scored more than 250 goals in his career and was a fantastic finisher, and I used to pick his brains in training and watch him. He was superb with both feet and scored goals not only for Hull but for the likes of Aberdeen, Leeds and Sheffield United. He was a great role model to try to emulate and it's amazing to think I eventually got more career goals than him.

Football was a bit different in those days and there were no big-time charlies, as you got put in your place straight away; but we had a really good side who were always up there challenging and most of them had been apprentices and had come through from the reserves, so it was a good place to be at that time; while Burnley, on the other hand, had gone right down the pan and were struggling in Division Four.

My debut was against Leeds and, as they were I think third at the time and we were around sixth, it was a big game, so it was switched to Sunday. Peter Swan, who of course went on to play for Burnley, played for Leeds in that game and, though he scored, we beat them 3-1.

I had scored loads of goals for the reserves by then, but obviously this was different; yet I scored within a minute, which relieved the pressure. It was just great to get a goal straight away in a big game like that and get my first-team career off to such a great start.

I had been told a couple of days before that I was playing and had a couple of sleepless nights because, all of a sudden, instead of playing in front of 200 I would be playing in front of 15,000. It was a massive game and a bit of a derby as well, and my mum and dad were coming across to watch, so I was really worrying about doing well because at that age any kind of criticism is really hard to take and if you are having a bad game the crowd will soon let you know.

As I said, we won the game and I scored, which was brilliant; but I came crashing back down to earth on the Monday when the manager, Brian Horton, straight away accused me of getting all 'Billy Big Time'. I wasn't, of course, but it was just his way of making sure I kept my feet on the ground.

Ironically, it was Keith Edwards I replaced, but he was coming to the end of his career then, while I was the 19-year-old young gun who was scoring goals left, right and centre in the reserves. I was really fit at the time; I'd win any running exercise in training. I was keen as mustard, so I don't think Keith could have had any complaints.

It was hard stepping up to the first team, because you knew you had to do the business, and you also had to get used to staying in hotels when you played away, as opposed to the reserves, when you just turned up in the mini-bus, played and went home. Also, your wages went up if you signed a new deal and you might actually have people asking for your autograph, which had never happened to me before.

I won the club's Young Player of the Year award and ended up top scorer, which was great, because it's always hard when you break into the first team, as so many players do, and do OK for a while then just fade out of football because they can't handle it.

I always had a single room when we played away. I used to get slaughtered for that, but the reason was because, after a long journey, I liked to be on my own and relax. I have roomed with players before, but they might be watching telly till two in the morning and you couldn't get to sleep. I always preferred to have my evening meal, then go to bed. I think they all thought I was a funny bastard, but I just liked my sleep when I wanted to go to sleep.

That continued all through my career and it was fine because there was always a spare room. I didn't need a mate to go and have a long chat with because, at end of the day, after a long coach journey, you were knackered anyway.

Brian Horton used to have a tradition where if the first team got beaten on the Saturday, he'd arrange a game against the reserves on the Monday and he would come in the reserves' dressing room and say: "Right, places up for grabs. They've got beat again."

Those games were always real kicking matches and were really hard, because if you started doing well against someone who was marking you, particularly if it was an old pro, they'd make it really, really difficult. Everyone was thinking of themselves, as you'd expect, and if I scored a couple of goals and was making the guy marking me look stupid, he'd let me know about it.

There were times when it got as far as fisticuffs and Brian Horton even used to encourage it. He would say: "No one's barred, get stuck in. I want to see a winner." Those reserves versus first team games were unbelievable. We were kicking lumps out of each other and it was just like a park game sometimes.

I must admit, I always used to be a bit gobby. If you're small, I think you've got to be cocky and stand up for yourself. But I used to get kicked and many a time I'd set myself up for a fight against someone I'd no chance of beating and got decked a few times. But you just got up and got on with it. It just became part and parcel of the game because, at the end of the day, you have to look after yourself first and foremost. If you're in the team, everything is hunky-dory for you; but it also means, if you're in, someone else isn't, and they might be a really popular player, so it's always a real dog-eat-dog situation.

But I got on with most of the lads; maybe because if things are going well everyone gets on with you, but I also had a lot of run-ins with other players.

I heard that Dean Windass wrote in his book that, when I got into the first team, I was walking round like a big-time charlie, apparently, which is absolute bullshit. Dean was a great player and a great lad, but when you get released, you sometimes get bitter and twisted. He was a local lad, Hull born and bred, and he ended up coming back to the club and doing an absolutely brilliant job, scoring close to 100 goals for them.

The jealousy between apprentices is unbelievable and they can play cruel tricks. I remember lads arranging to meet me on a Saturday night for a pint, but when I got to the pub, there would be nobody there and they were at the other side of the pub watching me standing there like a muppet.

Windass was the ringleader. As I said, Deano was a local lad and very popular, and obviously I was just that gobshite from Burnley with a funny accent, and he and the lads made it very difficult for me.

Once you actually settle into the first team, the fans take over and it doesn't matter whether people like you or not, because they will back you; but at that time it was a really vicious situation and Brian Horton and Dennis Booth would encourage it.

Horton would say: "We are going to do some training today and you are going to have a race round the track." They had a track at Hull where you'd do around 10 laps in a 12-minute run, and he'd say, "I want to see a winner", and would sit in a stand watching us all trying to out-do each other.

There were lads being released all the time. One lad had only been a pro six months and held a big party for his 18th, which everyone at the club went to; then, six months later, he was released and out of a job.

The day I signed as a pro, I remember ringing my mum and dad and telling them the good news, but I didn't have time to enjoy it because Horton was always putting the pressure on. Just two days later, I played in a reserve game and wasn't doing that well, and he pulled me over at half-time in front of everyone and said: "Are you taking the piss? Because I'll tell you what, I'll rip that fucking contract up now."

I think he was doing it just to bring me back down to earth, but it showed how intense the pressure was and how he was always on your case. At the end of the day, you just go out and do your best and some games you are going to have a nightmare, but some players just couldn't handle that side of him.

Brian Horton brought me through from when I was just a kid and he knew everything about me. He just knew when you weren't trying and he made it his business to know everything about you. Some managers don't get involved, but he certainly did and we were all shit-scared of him. I know I certainly was, because he was a really aggressive player and manager and he terrified me and the lads at times.

Dennis Booth was his sidekick, but he was more of a funny guy and it was like the old good-cop-bad-cop scenario, but Dennis could give it you as well when he wanted to.

Yet it was Brian who was really terrifying and if you ever gave him any back-chat you were down the road: it was as simple as that. When we were apprentices, one lad took a training top home, and Horton got us all together and said: "Right, there's a top gone missing. If none of you are going to admit it, whoever's taken it, just bring it back and leave it on that table." So the lad brought it in and put it on the table, and Brian came straight down and said: "Right, who's nicked it?" Nobody said anything, so he got us all in individually and found out who it was and sacked the lad.

Sometimes his half-time team talks were absolutely mental. He would throw stuff about and he'd be frothing at the mouth and generally going ape-shit. If one of our opponents was taking the piss, he'd say: "Go and break his fucking legs."

In one reserve game, I was playing alongside him and there was a clash of heads and he got a cut, and he went ballistic. He was coming off and he wanted to sort this guy out and he was saying to the lads: "Fuck him over, someone." He was just unbelievably aggressive, but you could get away with it in those days.

On the other hand, you could say he was unbelievably passionate. If we had a five-a-side on a Monday morning and he was playing, he wanted to win at all costs, to the point where you were running your bollocks off to make sure you won if you were on his side.

He would give you praise if it were due, but not overly praise you, because he's always one ahead. He didn't like players who he thought had let things go to their heads, so he would bring you crashing back down to earth immediately, which I think at that particular time was probably good.

But when you did get it, I guess it must have been worse than the old Ferguson hairdryer treatment. There were times when we'd been hammered and he gave us a right bollocking, and you found yourself going home thinking, "I can't believe this has just happened"; but you just had to get on with it. Football has its ups and downs and you can't be the hero every week.

Some of the younger players just couldn't handle it,

though. We signed a lad called Tim Hotte from non-league North Ferriby, and he actually played a few games in Hull's first team. Every training session, we used to have an exercise where, if you gave the ball away, you went into a circle in the middle of the field. Tim kept giving it away and he was in the middle all the time and it got so bad he couldn't handle the circle; he ended up packing in at the club because it looked like he nearly had a nervous breakdown as a result of all the stick he was getting. It must have been on his mind all the time and he couldn't even knock a simple ball that I saw; I guess the pressure had become so intense.

There was one occasion I nearly got stitched up. When I broke into the first team, a few of the senior pros said to me: "You want to get in and see the manager. You are doing really fucking well. Go and ask him for a rise." It was all 'wink, wink' to get me to go in. I didn't know it at the time, but the manager was in on it too. So, after a while, I knocked on the door and went in.

"What do you want?" said Horton.

"Well, I'm only on £70 a week and, well, I've broken into the first team, so what about a rise?"

You can probably guess what happened next.

He said: "Get out of this fucking office now before I swipe you," and when I got outside, the others were all pissing themselves because they'd set me up. And no, he didn't say, "only joking, come back in and have a new contract".

Only when you start scoring regularly in the first team do you really have the upper hand. Then you know the fans want you to stay and the manager's job might be on the line, so the pressure's on them to give in.

We had some great tours when we were at Hull, and the tour to Bermuda was probably the most memorable. It was a fantastic trip. We played the Bermudans and beat them 4-0 and I scored, but the main memory was of such a beautiful island and a brilliant place, which made it such a great experience.

We were only there for about 10 days, but it was my birthday during that time, so we arranged a night out. But the players stitched me up again, because they set up a drinking game where everybody downed a shot, except mine were loaded big time with vodka, but they were just drinking water. Of course, I got absolutely arseholed.

We had a big centre-half called Peter Skipper, who was a massive 6ft 2in bloke with a nose that had been broken a few times and who played about 400 games for us. I started getting fly with him when I was pissed, so he head-butted me and nearly knocked me out, and the lads just took me to my room and put me to bed. I remember waking up in the morning with spew everywhere and the realisation they had set me up again. That was just one of the occasions I was put in my place.

Another instance involved big Billy Whitehurst, the striker who was an absolute legend at Hull and the hardest man I have ever come across inside or outside football. He was about 15 stone, built like a brick shit-house and was rock hard. I was shit-scared of him, but when I played up front with him it was great, because he'd create havoc and make space for me and I'd pick up the pieces.

On this occasion, we'd had a really hard training session and I'd got in the big communal bath we used and I was just lying there. Billy and a couple of the other players had got in and I had my eyes shut because I was just so knackered. Billy came alongside me and had a shit right next to me. I didn't know, as I still had my eyes shut as this big log floated up alongside me. Everyone had got out of the bath and Billy was just sitting there when I opened my eyes and turned to look at this log.

"What the fucking hell is that?" I shouted and jumped out of the bath. Billy was so hard I just had to laugh it off, because to be honest he would have twatted me if I hadn't started laughing. Looking back now, it was quite funny, I suppose, but it just shows what it was like with Billy. When I played alongside him, he was so hard that, if he made a mistake, I always had to agree it was my fault.

When he went to Newcastle, he played in the same team as Paul Gascoigne and I think Gazza wrote in his book that he once nutmegged him in training and thought, "Fucking hell, what have I just done?", because Billy was after lynching him for that. He is a legend in Hull and he was a brilliant striker as well. He was hard but 100 per cent wholehearted and he'd get you goals. He was a battering ram, but brilliant for a young striker to play alongside.

We had some other good strikers, such as Dave Bamber and Keith Edwards, but Billy was fantastic. I'd gamble on all his flicks, but he could play as well, and could hold the ball up, and if there was anything in the box he'd attack it. He's a legend, as any Hull fan will tell you.

Brian, I suppose, was a father figure at the time and though very intense he was a brilliant manager who really made me as a footballer, so it was a shock when he was sacked. But I was in the first team by then, so I just got on with it, and we then had a succession of managers with Terry Dolan, Eddie Gray and Colin Appleton, who has since passed away, all having spells in charge.

Eddie Gray became my agent after he was sacked by Hull. He obviously knew clubs would be coming in for me after I got 18 goals in the year I broke into the first team and then 25 in my second year. I thought it was really glamorous at the time to have an agent, but that wasn't really the case.

Colin Appleton had a weird management style because he actually spoke in riddles. When he gave a team talk, you didn't really know what he was talking about and he became a bit of a laughing stock, though I don't mean that in a horrible way.

One day, Billy Whitehurst was in the dressing room when Colin was giving a team talk, but he was talking absolute rubbish and Billy just stood up and said: "This is bullshit, this is". Billy walked up and pushed Colin, who fell in the skip we used to put all the kit in. Billy just walked out of the dressing room and we were all looking amazed, and Colin just picked himself up out of the skip and carried on as if nothing had happened. He was a lovely fellow, but you just didn't know what he was talking about, in my opinion.

He only lasted about four months at Hull before he was

sacked. It's a results game at the end of the day, but Colin was a great guy who had been a really good player and who played for Leicester in an FA Cup Final; it's just that we didn't know what the hell he was on about.

Every time a new manager comes in, they always have a little bit of a shuffle and then you get players who were playing regularly all of a sudden finding themselves in the reserves. Obviously, they don't like it, as it is really hard at a football club unless you are in the first team.

Every manager changes things, but when Stan Ternent came in he brought a lot of players to the club, so there was a lot of competition for places and always somebody looking to take your place.

Ternent then took over and he was a massive influence on me; but unfortunately they didn't give him long enough, for some reason. He kept us up and then, at the beginning of the following season, when we were doing OK in mid-table, they sacked him. It was a crazy decision, because Stan was an absolutely brilliant coach.

Brian Horton and Stan were both very similar in that they were both winners and really intense characters; but in my opinion Stan was the better coach. I learned more from him than I did from anyone else, and I would even say Stan was the best coach I've ever worked with in the game.

Chapter 2 – Leaving Burnley Behind

When I started at Hull as a 16-year-old, we played in the Northern Intermediate League, which was played on Saturday mornings. It included the likes of Newcastle, Sunderland, Leeds, Sheffield United and Sheffield Wednesday, so, as you might guess, it was a very good league and a very hard one to play in. We were up against apprentices from all those clubs on a league basis and it represented my introduction to playing against good teams from other professional clubs.

There were some great players coming through at that time. For instance, Paul Gascoigne played for Newcastle against us. They were probably the best team around then, and they went on to win the FA Youth Cup in 1985. Gazza stood out as an unbelievable talent, but obviously he didn't play much in the Northern Intermediate League team because he was promoted to the first team at a young age and never looked back from there.

There wasn't just Gazza, though. There were so many other good players, such as David Batty at Leeds and Brian Deane at Sheffield United. When Batty was 16 years old, he seemed to be about 4ft 5ins and looked like he weighed about 3 stone, but he basically just went round topping people and getting away with it. He was a good player, though, and

The English Schools' Football Association

Arthur Rice, General Secretary:
4a Eastgate Street, Stafford ST16 2NQ Tel: 0785 51142

This is to certify that .. ..ANDREW..PAUL..PAYTON.. .. ..

has been registered as an Associated Schoolboy with

.. ..BURNLEY......... .. Football Club

This registration is subject to the terms of Football League Regulation 42

Registration Number

7770/205 . ....

A Rice .

Date of issue. .4..10..82 .. ..

General Secretary

'The start of my life as a footballer at Hull City'
(Courtesy of Lancashire Telegraph newspaper)

'Padiham St Johns - Hartley Cup Final Team'
(Courtesy of Lancashire Telegraph newspaper)

'A medal that I never knew was possible, so pleased to celebrate with my home town club'

Telephone: 27777/8 and 38021/2/3

BURNLEY FOOTBALL CLUB

(The Burnley Football & Athletic Co., Ltd.)

Company Registration No. 54222 England

Registered Office & Ground

TURF MOOR,
BURNLEY,
LANCS.

Manager: B. G. MILLER
Secretary: R. BRADSHAW

Chairman: J. E. JACKSON, Esq.

Our Ref: RB/WH

24th November, 1982

Mr. A. P. Payton,
7, Kings Drive,
HAPTON,
Nr. Burnley.

Dear Andrew,

I have pleasure in enclosing your registration slip in respect of you having signed as an Associated Schoolboy for this Club.

I look forward to meeting you in the near future.

Yours sincerely,

R. Bradshaw

R. Bradshaw,
SECRETARY.

Telephone: 27777/8 and 30021/2/3

BURNLEY FOOTBALL CLUB

(The Burnley Football & Athletic Co., Ltd.)

Company Registration No. 54123 England

Registered Office & Ground

TURF MOOR,
BURNLEY,
LANCS.

Manager: F. CASPER
Secretary: R. BRADSHAW

Chairman : J. E. JACKSON, Esq.

Mr. A. P. Payton,
7, Kings Drive,
Hapton,
Nr. Burnley.

18th May 1983.

Dear Andrew,

In accordance with the provisions of Football League Regulations I have pleasure in informing you that your name has been included in our list of players whose services we wish to retain next season.

With kind regards and looking forward to seeing you again next season.

Yours sincerely,

R. Bradshaw,
SECRETARY.

when he filled out later on he turned into a great player and of course went on to play for England.

When I first went to Hull, my digs were basically lodgings and the landlady was a lovely lady in her sixties called Rose Oliver. She really looked after me and became my second mum in a way.

Rose was a nice woman and I couldn't fault her. It was the days before mobile phones, so my mum had to ring her house phone to get hold of me and Rose would always pass messages on - she must have answered the phone to my mum hundreds of times.

She smoked like a chimney and liked a drink a bit too much, though. She drank Emva Cream, which she disguised by putting it in her milk. Sometimes, I'd hear her having full conversations, even though there was no-one else in the room; and other times, she'd make a salad for me before I'd even set off for training, so by the time I got back to eat it, it was terrible.

A lad called Laurie Pearson, who ended up playing in the first team, also stayed there for a while, as did a succession of triallists; but it wasn't great for them, as it was just a basic council house and the food was terrible.

The club was so skint in those days, they used to pay £30 a week for me to stay there, and that was all Rose would get. I was no different, as I was on the YTS scheme. My colleagues who lived at home with their mum and dad might have had a few quid, but people like myself who were in digs were absolutely potless all the time. Remember, there were no proper win bonuses or anything like that in those days.

It was ludicrous. We might get an extra quid or so if we won in the reserves, but it was next to nothing. Even in the first team, which was playing at the same level as the present-day Championship, we were only on something like a £30 win bonus.

Digs at Rose's were known as the dungeon - no one wanted to stay in them. They'd say, "you're not at Rose's, are you??". But I ended up staying there for a few years: it was poor, the standard of food was bad and also the house was just so basic. I think it was council house. When I look back, it's amazing: we had nothing - none of the lads did really, at that time.

As I said before, it was hard getting mates and keeping mates, because everything you did revolved around the football club and as there were 10 of you going for two places, it was very much a dog-eat-dog situation.

There were plenty of good lads there, such as the previously mentioned Dean Windass and Neil Buckley, and also Lee Jenkinson, who was eventually sold to Coventry for a half million pound transfer fee. You got to know them all well, but then you'd move on and lose touch, as is often the case in football.

To be honest, we worked that hard there was very little spare time, because when we were apprentices, even when we weren't training, we were cleaning the ground. We really worked hard at Hull; we were too tired to do much in our spare time. We certainly didn't do any drinking or anything like that, because the manager, Brian Horton, was very much against anything like that.

Brian Horton wasn't interested in our parents, either. We had one lad who came over from Burnley called Kieran O'Neill, who actually ended up signing for the Clarets as an apprentice. One day, he ended up being linesman in a practice match and when he told his parents on the phone that night, his dad rang Horton to complain. The next day, Horton called him in and said: "If your Dad ever rings me again, you are fucking out." Anyway, the lad, who was only 16, just ended up jacking it in because Horton had upset him so much.

We did get out for a drink sometimes, though, but we had to keep our heads down, because Hull was a rough town. As well as the football, there is a rugby league team called Hull Kingston Rovers and some very good amateur teams also, so there are a lot of very fit, very big lads about.

The birds always wanted a bit of you if you were a footballer and some of the lads would go home with anything, but you always had to be careful when you were out. One night, I had no taxi fare, so I walked home and I got chased on three separate occasions on that same walk home. The first occasion, a group of lads just started chucking bricks while I was about 100 yards in front of them, so when I turned the corner I set off running and outpaced them. Then, about another half mile down the road, a couple of blokes on the other side of the road started giving me a bit of the old "What you looking at?", so I had to run away again. Finally, a group of lads in a takeaway near me started giving me some grief, so I had to get away again. I never wanted any trouble, so I was shitting myself, and that night showed me in no uncertain terms how rough Hull was.

Brian Horton was boss when I made my debut in 1988, but

he was sacked and, after Colin Appleton took over, we had a nightmare and were bottom of the league.

Horton, who was player/manager to begin with, was, as I said, an absolute winner, but really strict and dominant. You knew what you were getting with Brian Horton and if you didn't do the business, he would tell you in no uncertain terms.

Back when I was in the youth team, when I was about 16, I had a problem with answering back to the referee and getting sent off, which happened about three times in only around 10 games. Horton gave me such an unbelievable bollocking to the point where he said: "If you get sent off again, you're sacked."

I got sent off one game and probably the referee said to me: "If you open your mouth one more time, I'll send you off" and I went "ah ah" and he sent me off. I really shouldn't have got sent off for that, but Brian Horton was on my case big style and he used to go mental after games. If we were losing, he'd come in and throw stuff around, and say things like: "If that player's dominating you, why are you letting him take the piss? Break his fucking legs; he's putting food on his table, you're not." He always encouraged really serious battling for places, which made the Monday first team v reserve games cut-throat stuff; but one thing about Brian Horton was that he knew the game inside out and he was a winner, so I have so much respect for him.

The late Colin Appleton, God bless his soul, was captain of Leicester in the 1969 FA Cup Final, so he had been a great player; but what I found with Colin was that he spoke in riddles and we didn't know what he was on about half of the time.

Once, in training, he said to a lad called Lee Warren, who came from Leeds: "What are you doing talking while I'm giving a team talk?"

He said, "I wasn't", and Appleton said, "Yeah you were, you silly cunt."

Lee said: "Why have you called me a cunt?", and he replied, "Because you are one."

I thought he was just a very strange fellow.

Then Eddie Gray came in and he was a fantastic player/manager. Eddie would join us in training and his left foot was like a magic wand. He was similar to Liam Brady. He was also a fitness fanatic and teetotal, and a brilliant guy, but unfortunately he just couldn't get the results.

Eddie ended up being my agent when he got the sack and he signed me up straight away because he obviously knew more than me and knew that clubs were coming in for me. He didn't railroad me into it, but the bottom line is that I signed and basically you are signing over a 12.5 per cent signing-on fee for nothing, so he knew what he was doing. But I have got great respect for him because he was a great guy, a legend as a footballer and he was a good manager.

Stan Ternent, who had been at Crystal Palace, then came in and it was the first time I'd actually come across Stan as a manager. He basically kept us up, but my goals had a lot to do with it.

Then, unfortunately, the following season, though I got 25

goals, we were in a relegation position and Stan was sacked. To be fair to him, it was a tough division with no money to spend.

I knew Stan's sons through going out in Burnley and I knew what a good coach he was straight away. He helped me develop a lot more than any other manager; he was a fantastic coach. When he kept us up, he brought new players in and got rid of the old wood, very similar to what he did when he came to Burnley. At Turf Moor, he kept us up; then, within two years, we were in the Championship - so I don't need to say much more on Stan.

On one occasion, we played Ipswich at home in an evening game and we were 3-0 up at half time and cruising, but Ipswich were a decent side at the time and pulled it back to 3-3. Then with the last kick of the game I made it 4-3. But Stan had turned into the Incredible Hulk during that game. He was going absolutely spare, so when we won it at the death, I was thinking: "Oh my God, I'm glad I've scored", because I knew we were going to get a right roasting from Stan.

He was from the same school as Brian Horton, where, if you hadn't played well, you knew you were going to get bollocked. Stan wanted 100 per cent and if you didn't give that you were in for it; but tactically he was very good and I would say he had a massive influence on my career.

When Stan unfortunately got the sack at Hull, Terry Dolan came along and what can I say about him? Bland is the word, I think. He was like a headmaster and I think he gave me the impression he had no fire in his belly. He was well organised, but he was maybe what I imagine Sven Goran Eriksson to be like: more of a school teacher than a manager.

He had a sidekick with him called Geoff Lee, who was his assistant, and they had a 'good cop, bad cop' routine, but he wasn't much of a bad cop, certainly not in Stan or Brian's class. Basically, then, the club had set its sights on becoming mediocre, because unfortunately that's what they both were, in my opinion. I'm not having a big go at them or anything like that, because they were OK guys, but I personally just didn't rate them as coaches.

We had some good players at Hull during my time there, such as Gary Parker, who also played for Nottingham Forest and Aston Villa, and there was a lad called Billy Askew, who went to Newcastle for £250k, and of course Billy Whitehurst, who also went to Newcastle.

We also had Nicky Barmby training with us at the time. He chose Tottenham instead of Hull, but he is back at his home town club now.

It was a really good set-up at Hull, where they looked after the players and proof of the pudding was that at least seven players from the YTS scheme got into the first team, and that is a huge amount.

I can remember another great memory. I'd been to New Zealand, but when I came back to Hull, we had a great FA Cup run in the 1989-90 season. We went through to the quarter-finals, where we got a plum home tie against that great Liverpool side of the time.

Boothferry Park was packed to the rafters to see us take on a team containing the likes of John Aldridge, Steve McMahon,

Ian Rush, Ronnie Whelan and John Barnes, with of course Bruce Grobbelaar in goal.

Incredibly, though we were only a mid-table second-tier side, we were 2–1 up at half time, with Billy Whitehurst and Keith Edwards getting the goals. I remember playing on the right wing and not really touching the ball that much, but it was just unbelievable being 2-1 up against an absolutely awesome team.

The crowd were going delirious at half-time because we were expected to get absolutely annihilated, and we were just 45 minutes from the semi-finals, which would have been unbelievable. But in those days the big clubs always played their strongest team and you always felt a team of that calibre would come back at you. We ended up losing 3-2, with Aldridge scoring near the end; but it was a fantastic experience against a team that went on to go through the awful trauma of the Hillsborough Disaster in the semi-final before eventually winning the FA Cup.

The young left back, David Burrows, was marking me and he was a decent player. Liverpool were so hard to play against because they kept the ball so well and we were doing well just to get a touch at some point, so it was a big learning curve; but with a massive crowd and a televised game, it was still a wonderful experience.

I was subbed late on, but I hadn't had much impact on the game at all, to be honest; but it was just a fantastic Liverpool team right through which had class written all over it and it was daunting playing against them because obviously that was one of the first times in my career that I'd ever played against such huge stars. I didn't do much that day because I was too overawed, but I think I learned a lesson that day, because certainly at Celtic and at other future clubs, I worked out that you have to get on with it and not be too overawed by big names.

As I said, I was on the wing that day, as I was for most of my first 50 games for Hull. I scored all my goals at reserve level as a striker, but I think, because of my size and because we had Billy Whitehurst and Keith Edwards, who at the time were two excellent strikers, I was played out wide in the first team.

But I knew I would always get goals and in my first full season in the first team I got 18, even though I played out wide. I'd always get in the box when the ball was on the other side, because I knew I was a striker anyway, so I'd always be in there to try to get those goals. It's just a striker's instinct.

I had a great time at Hull overall, though. I made my debut in 1988 and scored. I really had three full seasons of first-team football. I bagged 18 goals in my first full season, 25 the following term and then I'd got around 13 in around a dozen my last season before I went to Middlesbrough. I ended up with 57 goals in total for Hull, 50 of which were in the old Division Two, which is the equivalent of today's Championship; so, all in all, that's not a bad record.

I never played against Burnley for Hull, which I am glad about. As soon as I started scoring in the first team, every time I went home I used to get all this, "I was better than you at school", and it made it worse because everybody knew I'd been released by Burnley. I used to get a lot of that.

And I'll tell you something. There's no way I was going to go out in Burnley that night after I scored the winner for Barnsley. I would have been a glutton for punishment and somebody would have definitely thrown one at me. In any case, I wouldn't have gone out anyway, as it would have seemed like gloating; so I made sure I was well out of the way that night.

When I was about 18, I'd go out now and again on Saturday night in Hull and one of those nights, I met a beautiful girl called Suzanne Clark. She had blonde hair and was really, really nice looking. She took a bit of a shine to me, so I started going out with her. I was seeing her on and off for about six months, but only casual dates, such as going to the pictures and things like that.

I lost touch when I went home to Burnley for the summer holidays, but when I got back to Hull, I read in the papers that she'd been a passenger in a car which had been in a bad crash and she was in a really bad way. I went round to her house, but all the curtains were closed and her brother answered the door. I asked if I could see her in hospital, but he politely said they were only allowing family visitors. But I decided to go anyway and when I got there I could see she was on a life-support machine.

Her mum was there and she was OK about me visiting and thanked me for coming. I started to go and see her on a regular basis and she slowly improved, and eventually came out of hospital, even though she was still in a bad way and had to have physio each day because her head injuries had been so bad.

I was doing well at Hull and had broken into the first team and was scoring goals, and one thing led to another and after about six months we got married. Looking back, it was crazy really, because we were just kids, and I remember my dad saying, "Do you know what you are doing?"

Then our son Charley came along. He was actually born in Middlesbrough, as I'd been transferred there when she was heavily pregnant. Soon afterwards, I went to Celtic, so she was even further away from her family. She got to go home one week a month and it got to the stage where I was glad when she was going home and so was she, so the marriage just fizzled out. I realised I didn't love her and vice versa, and I think it was more of a mutual thing.

Charley was always going to go with his mum, but it was soul destroying at the time because then he was my only child and my son. I would try to get back to see him in Hull, but it would be fleetingly, maybe once a month for a Saturday night. However, I got to see him more when I went to Barnsley and got into a routine where I was seeing him once every two weeks. I would bring him over to Burnley and he'd stay for the weekend, but it was hard because he lived with his mum and he went to school in Hull. We did have a father-son relationship, but when his mum met someone else and got remarried, things changed, because he didn't want to come over any more.

I can't deny the break-up with Charley's mum affected me on the football pitch, even though that's always the place where you can try and put any off the field problems behind you.

Like a lot of other players, I'll admit I've not had a problem-free career - drink-driving convictions and things like that - and, though the football pitch is where you do tend to feel you can be free of any worry, it's hard to blank things out completely. If you have got problems, you have got problems. Thankfully, I've never had any major problems, but it is hard, especially when you come back to Burnley.

Everyone knows you and wants to know what you're about, so if they see you out once, they'll say straight away: "He's a pisshead, I've seen him out". Now that is just because someone has seen you in a pub. It doesn't matter if you've had 10 pints or you've had an orange, that's how it works.

Back to events on the pitch, and things were going well for me. But there is one massive difference playing in the reserves in comparison to the first team which I had to get used to, and that's the fact that, in the reserves, there's virtually no crowd. Therefore, when you finally score a goal in the first team, you really don't know how to react or celebrate when the crowd goes mad.

I remember making my first-team debut for Hull and that Sunday derby game at home to Leeds United. There were 15,000 people there and I fortunately scored within a minute in a game we eventually won 3-1. I remember thinking how weird it felt and wondering what I should do to celebrate in front of all those people, when I was used to scoring in front of a handful of spectators in the reserves. I thought: "What do I do? How do I celebrate?" I ended up running to the crowd with my arms in the air in the middle of this fantastic noise.

That's when you get a taste for it, when you hear the roar of the crowd. If you're scoring goals in that great atmosphere amid all the tension and pressure of playing in front of a big crowd, it's just great. That's what I love about football.

But the downside is the pressure. That's the hardest part, because obviously you are expected to do it every game and that is impossible for anybody.

We played at some great stadiums when I was at Hull. We were up against Manchester United at Old Trafford in a cup game, which was a great experience, even though we lost 5-0 and I was an unused sub. We also played at Everton and Aston Villa, and you get even more of a taste for professional football when you go to places like that with such great facilities and top-class dressing rooms.

Other grounds were great experiences for other reasons. For instance, playing Millwall at the Old Den was amazing. They had some great players like Teddy Sheringham and Terry Hurlock and were an unbelievable team, but they used to get a lot of crowd trouble there and it was a scary place to go. You were in a constant state of fear, even when you were actually on the pitch, because the crowd were so intimidating.

Then there were places such as Doncaster who, at their old ground, had nothing facility-wise, though we didn't have great facilities at Hull, to be fair. We were used to having nothing, so anything else was sort of a bonus.

One of the most memorable goals I scored for Hull was in a 5-2 home win over Brighton. I bagged two that day, but the one I remember was when I got the ball out wide, as I started the game playing on the right wing. It was highlighted in the local paper how I got the ball deep in my own half and went on a mazy run, beating four or five players.

Yet I must admit a lot of my goals were tap-ins, and also a fair proportion of them were penalties. I always liked taking penalties and never turned down the chance to take one, because, when you think about it, it's an easy chance to score another goal. However, I only got one penalty when I was at Hull because they had a regular spot-kick taker in Leigh Palin, a good player who went on to turn out for Bradford City and Port Vale.

At Hull, I had scored 43 goals in two seasons for a club that was struggling for much of the time, so everybody thought I was going to be sold in the summer of 1990. I had just scored 25 league goals for a Hull side that had been relegated from the second tier of English football and I was still only 22, so a lot of clubs were looking at me.

But the Tigers held out, because they wanted a big fee for me; so I ended up starting the new season still with the club in what is now Division One. I had a few hamstring problems at the beginning of that season and I only played about eight games, but I scored about eight goals and there was still speculation about a move.

I did not have many injuries, but ONE of the most harrowing incidents of my career was when Hull played Oldham at Boundary Park in the early 1990s, in what would now be called the Championship, when the home side had that controversial artificial pitch.

I was up front and it had started raining quite heavily, so the surface was quite slippery. I was put clean through and their keeper, Jon Hallworth, came out and, as he did so, he slid and his foot went right under my chin. The next thing I can remember is waking up in Oldham Royal Infirmary two hours later. I had broken my jaw in two places and swallowed my tongue.

I had to have an operation where they wired up my jaw and it was clamped together. When you wake up in the morning, the first thing you do is yawn – and you can't open your mouth! You can't eat and you have to go on liquidised food, so it was pretty gruelling. I couldn't kick a ball for three months, which was obviously tough because I was 19 and had just broken into the first team. It was hard work because I couldn't train, and in fact couldn't do anything because any form of running would have been like pounding the jaw and would upset my recovery. In addition, my face swelled up like the elephant man and I'm not joking. My jaw was broken in two places, and the injury was so painful I couldn't sleep, so it was very nasty and certainly the worst injury I've suffered.

Yet I count myself very lucky because, at the time of the incident, the Hull physio, Geoff Radcliffe, saved my life. Apparently, my tongue started slipping back down my throat when I'd become unconscious and I probably would have died. Things like that certainly put everything else in perspective.

I was only 19 and had a very slight build anyway, but I still lost a lot of weight through having liquidised food for every meal for three months. It was like eating soup every meal, and when I finally got the wires off, my mum made me bacon and eggs and I got to chew something for the first time, which felt unbelievable.

It was a long road back and, sure enough, two minutes into my first training session when I returned, somebody toe-ended the ball straight in my face. It's Sod's Law for footballers. If you've got a broken toe, somebody will stand on it, won't they? Luckily, my jaw had healed properly, but I remember thinking what the consequences could have been and and I'm still shuddering!

I had only just broken into the side, having got 25 goals for the reserves, who had won the league, but after the injury I literally had to prove myself all over again. At the time I had been on about £70 a week with a one-year contract, and even when I signed a new contract I only went up to about £90 a week.

I fought my way back into the team, but at the time it was a dark period for the game with the Bradford fire and Heysel disaster and Hillsborough a few years later, and York City striker David Longhurst actually died on the pitch after suffering a heart attack. Things like that really hit home and, again, it puts the game in perspective.

I can remember going into the club just like any other day and the manager said Middlesbrough had come in and offered a club record fee of £750,000, rising to a million on appearances, which was a lot of money for Hull, who were struggling financially at the time. Lenny Lawrence was Boro manager at the time, so myself, my agent Eddie Gray and my dad went to meet Lenny and the Middlesbrough chairman at a hotel.

To cut a long story short, they were going to offer me a

£35,000 signing-on fee, then a grand a week pay. Then, if Middlesbrough got promotion to the Premier League, which looked likely as it was November and they were riding high in the league, I would get a £500-a-week rise.

Even so, I wasn't ready to sign immediately as I actually still thought a Premier League club would come in, which I still think they would have done if Hull and I had just held out for a bit longer. But I remember Lenny Lawrence saying to my dad, "Look, if he goes back to Hull now and breaks his leg in training tomorrow, all this financial security is gone", and so my dad said to me, "Go on, get it signed."

So I ended up signing a three-and-a-half-year deal with Middlesbrough. I think a lot of people were surprised because, even though they were a big-name club at the time, they thought I was going to go somewhere bigger. But when you get that sort of deal offered on a plate, it is difficult to turn down what amounts to financial security.

Chapter 3 Glad To Get Out

I couldn't play in Middlesbrough's first game because I didn't sign in time, but I was introduced at half-time on the pitch and interviewed; then the next week I was straight in for the home game against Bristol City. I thought I might be on the bench and they would stick with their regular front three of Bernie Slaven, John Hendry and Paul Wilkinson, but they left Slaven out. I scored two minutes into my debut and everyone was going mental because the press were raving and the fans were thinking they'd signed the next Kevin Keegan or something.

But then there was a really bad turn of events. I damaged my ankle ligaments just before half-time and was carried off. I was out for a couple of months, which was a nightmare because, in that time, the 'clique', as I'll call them, i.e. Slaven, Hendry and Wilkinson, became the regular front three again and they made it very difficult for me. Hendry in particular made it hard because he didn't want me playing, I suppose because I could score and his place was at risk.

I didn't have a particularly good time there off the pitch: I was always finding I was trying to chase friends, if you know what I mean. I didn't enjoy my time there at all.

I only played eight games for them in total. They had a great run in the cups, making the semi-final of what was then called the Milk Cup before losing to Manchester United and reaching the quarter-finals of the FA Cup, but I played no part as I was cup-tied for both competitions.

Yet I did get three vital league goals and we ended up getting promoted to the Premiership, beating Wolves 2-1 at Molyneux in the last game of the season to go up automatically in the year Blackburn went up in the play-offs. It was absolutely brilliant at the end because it was unbelievable getting to the top flight and all the players had a great togetherness, and we also got an £18k bonus each for going up, which also helped.

But when we got back after the summer, the same old problems started again with Hendry. He was a fly guy and I did not get on with him at all and wouldn't get on with him now if we met up. Then Celtic came in for me, which was ironic and superb from my point of view because Hendry was a big Celtic fan as well as being clown prince of the dressing room and chief piss-taker.

It was unusual how the move to Middlesbrough came about. Liam Brady, who's head of the Arsenal Academy now, was Celtic manager at the time and came down to Hull one weekend when Celtic didn't have a game and saw me score two against Darlington. Straight after the game, I went into the manager's office and heard he'd offered half a million pounds there and then. I was stood there in shock. This was Liam Brady, a legend who'd played for Juventus, Inter Milan and Arsenal, trying to sign me.

Anyway, to cut a long story short, they couldn't agree a fee, so I went to Middlesbrough, who went up at the end of that season.

But then, in the close season, I got a phone call out of the blue from Stan Ternent, saying he'd had a call from Liam Brady and he wanted me and that I was to go up for talks the following day. I had three years of my contract left at Middlesbrough and I hadn't heard anything from anybody, so I was a bit sceptical. My agent Eddie Gray's son Stuart was a pro at Celtic, so I thought surely Eddie must know if there's any interest, especially as he would be due his 12.5 per cent fee.

But Stan said: "When you go into work tomorrow, if the manager pulls you he is going to tell you about Celtic, but if nowt happens, you've not heard this from me, because they don't like to talk about it."

Anyway, right at the end of training the following day, as I was about to go home, I got pulled by the manager and he said Celtic wanted me and I was going up for talks at 9am the next day. So I have got to get hold of my agent and find out what he knows and whether I'm doing his job for him. So I called him.

"Hiya, Eddie, it's Andy Payton," I said.

"All right, son?" Eddie Gray replied.

"Have you heard owt about owt?"

"Nah. Why?"

"Because I'm going to Celtic in the morning for talks."

"What?"

"And you've got to come with me, because you're my fucking agent."

So he gave it a bit of flannel and tried to make out that he might have known about it, but he'd broken his wrist so he couldn't drive and my dad ended up offering him a lift. It was farcical. It just shows you don't know what you are going to get with agents.

Anyway, I'd never even been to Glasgow, never mind Celtic, before, so we'd no idea where we were going. We got to a mile away from Parkhead, but couldn't find the ground, even though we were frantically trying, and we eventually got there about half an hour late for talks, with Eddie Gray following behind us in a car driven by one of his other sons. We ended up asking directions from these two drunken blokes.

"Oy, mate. Where's Parkhead?" I said.

"Are you taking the piss?" he said, and I turned round and it was there over my shoulder, as big as Wembley Stadium.

So we finally got there and Liam Brady showed me round the ground. It was absolutely massive, unbelievable facilities, restaurants, all the history of the club everywhere to be seen. They were, of course, the first British club to win the European Cup and they had all the pictures up and a replica of the European Cup.

He had sold it to me immediately. I couldn't believe a club like that wanted me, to be honest, because I was at Hull nine months earlier.

The transfer was an exchange deal with an Irish international called Chris Morris, who was at Sheffield Wednesday for years when they were in the top flight, along with Derek White going the other way. The deal was valued at one and a half million.

I was only on a grand a week at Middlesbrough and basically I sat down in Brady's office and this guy was so laid back class was oozing out of him. Everybody at that time knew he was the most successful British player ever in Italy; he had captained Juventus and Inter and won pretty much every honour in the game.

"How are you doing, son?" he said.

"Yeah, I'm all right," I replied, obviously in awe of the great man.

"What are you on at Middlesbrough?"

"Er ..."

"What about £1,700? How does that sound?"

"Yeah, Yeah," I replied, and that was it.

Eddie Gray just sat there, even though he knew Liam as he had played against him, and it was obvious he had known nothing about the deal. Then Liam just said: "Right, son. I'll see you in the morning at training."

So me and my dad then went straight to the hotel Celtic had sorted for us, and my dad was loving it. It had a swimming pool and he said, "Right, I'll stay up here with you for a couple of days," and when I got back from training there he was in the pool and loving it.

I still couldn't believe I was a Celtic player and hardly slept that night, but I had to get ready for a press conference the day after, when they were unveiling myself and Stuart Slater, who they signed from West Ham for a record £1.8 million.

A lad called Rudi Vata, who was an Albanian international, was in the hotel with me and he couldn't speak any English whatsoever. He came down for breakfast and I sat opposite him, nodded and said, "Hiya, mate", and mumbled something, and he sort of went "Huh?", as he couldn't speak a word of English. But six months on, he could speak fluent English with a Scottish accent!

Chapter 4 Big Time Charlie

Celtic is a huge club and the facilities were fantastic and the stadium was massive. I signed straight away after the conversation with Liam Brady, but I wanted to go back to Middlesbrough to pick up my boots.

Clearly I'd been absent that day and no one knew where I was, especially Hendry, who had no idea what was happening. I remember walking into the dressing room and asking one of the apprentices to go and get my boots. Straight away, Hendry said: "Why? Where are you going?" I waited till the apprentice came back and all the players were there waiting, because nobody knew, and I said: "Right, I'm going. I'm going to Celtic." Hendry's face dropped and I just walked out of the dressing room, leaving him standing there absolutely gutted, bearing in mind I gave him the middle finger while I walked out. What a moment.

I'd only played eight games and scored three goals for Boro, and I was only there for nine months, and as they were still at their old ground, Ayresome Park, then, the facilities were basic and not much better than Hull's; so, to be honest, I was glad to get away from Middlesbrough and Hendry and couldn't wait to get to Celtic.

On my first day when I got in, there were internationals everywhere. There was Paul McStay, who was Scotland captain at the time; Garry Gillespie, who'd been a legend at Liverpool; Charlie Nicholas, who went on to Arsenal, of course; Frank McAvennie; John Collins; Tommy Boyd; a Polish lad called Darius Dubczyk, who won 50 caps; Peter Grant, who played almost 400 games for Celtic; and Tony Mowbray.

I found a big difference between them and the Middlesbrough lads. They were absolutely brilliant. Paul McStay was an absolute gentleman who straight away said: "Are you all right, pal? How is it going? Don't worry about it." He could probably see I was a bit scared at what lay ahead.

Then you go training and you know you either get with the programme or you are going to fade.

I went to Padiham St John's, which was a Catholic school, but I wasn't really a practising Catholic, and while I knew most Celtic players were of that faith, I was never actually asked if I was a Catholic or not when I signed for the club. I once scored a goal for Celtic and went over to the touchline where our fans were, and I heard one of them shouting to me to make the sign of the cross. I didn't take him on, and when you recall what happened to Paul Gascoigne when he pretended to play the Loyalist flute when he scored for Rangers, I probably made a wise move. There were threats to his life, I believe, after that, but he probably didn't even think about it and just saw it as a joke.

There was definitely a lot of sectarian singing at the time, which thankfully they are trying to sort out now, but it gave you a sense of the deep-rooted hatred and intensity which goes way beyond normal banter.

I don't think the Celtic fans really minded that I was English. You can be on a bit of a shaky one, but because I was doing the business for them, scoring in my second game and going on to do well, I was fine.

The history of the club was always very relevant, particularly of course the story of the legendary 'Lisbon Lions', who won the European Cup in 1967 with a team entirely composed of players born in and around the Glasgow area.

Bobby Lennox, who was one of the Lisbon Lions, was youth team coach and had actually come to watch me a few times at Hull when he was scouting for Liam Brady. He was a fantastic, brilliant guy with an unbelievable scoring record, bagging 273 goals for Celtic. I met Jimmy Johnstone and a few of the other greats, but Bobby I knew particularly well because he was on the coaching staff up there and I always found him a really excellent coach and he really helped me up there. He took me under his wing in a way and I had a lot of time for him.

Liam Brady had been a fantastic player, but he was under pressure as Celtic manager. However, in his favour, I have to stress we were up against an outstanding Rangers side with the likes of Ally McCoist, Andy Goram and Richard Gough, and though we beat them in an Old Firm game and I got the winner, they proved that, though we were good, they were better by winning the league, and it was no consolation for us to finish second.

There was always pressure on players up there and they scrutinise every training session; but it was worse for Stuart Slater, who came to the club from West Ham on the same day I joined from Middlesbrough. He was their record signing at the time at £1.8 million, so was under pressure anyway, but it got worse for Stuart, who was a good player. He was a winger but basically the press got on to the fact that he had not scored for ages. He had gone something like 50-odd games without a goal for West Ham and then Celtic and, as I was in the same hotel as him, I could see he really felt the pressure and his confidence went completely.

Stuart ended up going to Ipswich and there were rumours Liam Brady, who had been sacked by then, had sorted the move out to help him. It was a great shame, because Stuart was a good player and a tricky winger and a great lad, but I don't think he had the mental strength to cope with the intense pressure.

As I said, it was highly pressurised and you've got to imagine the scrutiny you are under up there. You have a press conference every day, so when you have finished training you don't go home, as at other clubs. Even the reserve games were covered by loads of press and they would always ask you leading questions to try to get anything they can to make into a headline.

When the players went on a night out, which wasn't that often, the press would be following us around! They were under cover and didn't have press cards in their hats or cameras round their necks, but the older players pointed them out and warned us.

They had these stunning girls with them and they would try to get them to sit on players' knees and get a photo. They would always try to set up the married ones, such as Paul

McStay. He was captain of Scotland and Celtic, and devoutly religious, a regular churchgoer who was married with kids. It was OK for us getting him bladdered around the pubs on our Christmas do, but these pressmen were always trying to get birds to sit on his knee to get that click, so the club had minders who were also under cover and who stayed with the group to keep an eye on us and made sure we were OK.

Victoria's in Glasgow was one place we would go to, and one night we had beaten FC Cologne 3-0 at home in a European game after losing 2-0 in Germany, so we went straight up to the Piano Bar at Victoria's to celebrate.

It was absolutely packed but, because it was so volatile up there, you never knew who had it in for you, so there were bouncers everywhere to protect us. Glasgow has got a really good side to it and a city culture, but it also has a violent side.

I loved it in Scotland, but obviously I can't argue the standard of football is as high as the Premier League. For example, a club like Kilmarnock or St Johnstone could never compete in the Premier League, in my opinion.

But there was still pressure because, if you are playing for Celtic or Rangers, even a draw away at Aberdeen is a bad result. You have to win every game and, when you get home gates of 60,000, you know there is no hiding place and you have got to do the business.

With their spending power and fanatical support, both at home and away, I think both Rangers and Celtic would survive in the Premiership and they would certainly fill every ground; but clubs like Motherwell and Hearts would not and would be Championship sides at best, in my opinion.

However, there were loads of great players in Scotland when I was there. Paul McStay was unbelievable, as I've said. He was captain of Scotland and a midfield player who would never give the ball away. John Collins, who played at Hibernian and went on to Celtic, then Monaco, won 58 Scottish caps and was also fantastic.

Frank McAvennie was still a great player and Charlie Nicholas was brilliant, even though he was coming to the end of his career. I could carry on. We had a winger called Joe Miller, who was a fantastic player, and there was also Gary Gillespie, Tony Mowbray and Tom Boyd, who played for Scotland more than 50 times.

Mowbray was one player I got to know quite well because he had been at Middlesbrough. He was a great guy, teetotal and a very dedicated player who was a great centre half and a captain and leader.

Tony met this girl who was fantastic and came to all the games. They found out she had cancer, but she fought it and they got married, but unfortunately the disease returned and she passed away. I went to the funeral, which was a very emotional and harrowing occasion. Tony did remarkably well to face that tragedy and continue his career, and he showed he is a strong character.

But he wasn't the only one to suffer personal tragedy. We had a striker called Tommy Coyne, who was a great lad and very popular. We went on a pre-season training camp in Italy as we did every year at the time and we got news that his wife sadly passed away in very tragic circumstances. It hit the team hard because Tommy was such a great guy and it was such a bolt from the blue. It was just a massive shock, but it brought the players closer together, as did the tragedy with Tony's wife, which came shortly afterwards.

At the time I was married but my son Charlie, who was born in Middlesbrough, lived back in Hull. The circumstances were that my girlfriend at the time, Sue, was involved in a serious car crash and we got married after that, but we both later accepted that we should never have got married as we were too young. They both came with me when I moved to Glasgow, but it didn't work out because Sue wanted to be back in Hull and I wanted to get on with my football career.

It came to a head when I was due to play in a reserve game against Rangers at Ibrox. Sue had moved up there, but she would go home for a week every month, and I would make sure she had a flight back to Humberside. But it wasn't working out big time and it was getting to the point of divorce anyway, and, on this occasion, I'd paid for her parents to come up on the plane and pick her up.

To cut a long story short, we had an argument and, because her parents were there, I left the scene and, rather than play in the reserve game as planned, I just jumped into my car, did not think and drove and ended back at my mum and dad's in Burnley. And on the motorway back down to England, I took my wedding ring off and threw it out of the car window.

The press jumped on the fact that I went AWOL straight away and, even though it was a reserve game, they slaughtered me for a while; but to be honest, my head was up my arse a little bit and I was feeling down.

I was back in training on the Monday and I explained what happened and the club weren't happy, even though it was only a reserve game. They said I should have told them if I was going through some problems and they would have helped. Anyway, I got back in training and was back in the squad the next Saturday and I think I scored. It can be very hard to focus on playing a game of football when something like that is happening, especially if the press are all over it. It's very tough, but you just have to get on with it as best you can.

Of course, we did end up splitting up and then getting divorced, and we never really saw each other after that, apart from in court, where the CSA ensured she got it all and I got nothing, which is the usual scenario as far as I'm concerned.

I think I signed for Celtic on the Thursday. I just thought: "Well, maybe I am going to be on the bench." We were playing Dundee Utd.

Anyway, I got pulled after training and the manager said: "Right, you are starting Saturday; Charlie Nicholas is sub."

I am thinking, "Oh, fuck me."

I was up front with Gerry Creaney, who was flying at the time. He was 21 and was as good as anything I've seen - he was outstanding. He went on to Manchester City and Portsmouth and scored a lot of goals. He had a spell at Burnley and scored a few goals there too. I think injuries affected him, but when he was younger he was superb.

I couldn't believe I was playing, so had a sleepless night the night before. After training, I attended the press conference, which was unbelievable. As when I signed for Middlesbrough, there were local press there, but at Celtic there was a roomful of media from all over the country.

I'd never experienced anything like match days there; it was such a huge event, with a massive crowd and ground. But the reception I got was unbelievable and we won 2-0. Creaney got both goals, but I had a good game, even though I didn't score. The fans were just unbelievable and what really struck me was a moment when it was still 0-0 and we got a corner and the crowd just erupted because they heard Rangers had conceded a goal. I didn't know what was going on, to be honest. In fact, the noise all through was just unbelievable and the atmosphere incredible.

People say a lot of things about the Scottish League, but I can tell you, you are under pressure when you put that green and white on because it is like a sacred jersey to the fans and football is a religion to them. There were even regularly 1,000 people turning up just to watch us train. At Hull there was one man and his dog, if you were lucky, so you had pressure on you even when you were training.

But what used to be really funny was that right near the training ground there was a factory and it was full of Rangers fans, so when we came out of the training ground, rain or shine, hail or snow, there would be about 500 of them stood outside waiting just to tell us to "fuck off" and give us the V's.

We would end up doing it back and they would all start cheering. They would be there every day, even Christmas Day. It was unbelievable; they would get piss-wet through standing there just to give you the V's and shout, "You fuckin' bastards". That's how intense it was up there.

All the players were brilliant and I got on with them all, but I was in the hotel with Frank McAvennie, so obviously I had a few nights out with him. Stuart Slater was also great, but they were all top lads. At Middlesbrough and smaller clubs, you get the John Hendry's of this world who like to rule the roost, but there was nothing like that at Celtic.

The following Tuesday, we played Dundee in the Cup and Brady put the same team out, and I scored the only goal. It was straight in the bottom corner past Jim Leighton, the great keeper who had played for Aberdeen and Manchester United. So, four days after signing I've got my first goal, the crowd are going mental and I'm on the crest of a wave, and I ended up top scorer that season.

But the thing that struck me most was the sheer size of the operation; from finishing training and going in the restaurant for something to eat to match days, it was just class.

One thing that did happen was that they had an initiation process up there and they did it to every new player. One of the centre halves was Mick Galloway, who was a big lad, about 6ft 2ins, and probably about 14 stone: a big, old fashioned centre half.

I was about 22 and very fast and one of the players pulled me over and said, "What are you like at sprinting 400 metres?" I said OK, but the player said, "Mick will beat you." Anyway, I looked at Mick and thought: "No, he won't."

I wondered if there was something going on, but then Mick came up and said: "What's all this you've been saying? That you'll beat me? I'll race you round the track then." So I said OK and by then they've got me hook, line and sinker.

Everybody goes out and watches, even the office staff, and the manager then comes out and says: "Right, we are timing it. You have got to go for it."

He shouted "Go!" and apparently what usually happened was that the player sets off and Mick runs a yard then turns back and doesn't move, and the player has gone 10 yards before he realises. But I went like the clappers with my eyes shut and had gone 200 metres before I realised. I got the biggest clap of all time because, when I was coming round the far turn and I looked across, they were all on their knees. They had never seen anyone run so far. I really fell for it, but it stood me in good stead, because they knew at least I was honest and I could take a joke.

They put me up in the best hotel in Glasgow, which had a swimming pool. As I've said, my Dad loved the pool, five-star restaurant, etc.

One of the most striking things I noticed was that, when I got into training at nine o'clock, there would be players already in the gym doing extra work before the training actually started. That's how dedicated they were and I realised quickly that was the sort of thing you had to do if you wanted to be an international. At a lot of clubs, you'd get players just sitting around reading the paper and farting about, but at Celtic, even the older players like John Collins were in the gym doing stuff. He would be on the parallel bars at nine in the morning and I'm talking doing 500 reps, then doing 500 sit-ups, and then be in the gym again after training.

A lot of those good things rubbed off on me, as I realised

doing that extra work just gave you that advantage, that edge over the opposition. When you're playing in front of crowds of 60,000, you know you've got to put everything into your training, because they will let you know if you are having a bad time.

We had a player called Jackie Dziekanowski, who was a Polish international and a bit of a playboy. He scored a lot of goals, but he was coming to the end of his time and ended up at Bristol City and did well for them. I stayed at his house once and it was unbelievable: a huge, four-bedroomed detached pad with a double garage, Jacuzzi, etc. I opened my window in the morning and there were people playing golf, because it was overlooking a course and right next to a fairway.

Liam Brady was a massive influence while I was there. He was still young enough to join in training and his left foot was a magic wand. He was unbelievable, but he was very laid back. He had the Italian influence in training morning and afternoon, as we did a lot of that, which I had never done before. At some clubs, you would go in, run your bollocks off and then go home; but this was a different mentality.

He was a good manager, but unfortunately for him he was up against probably the best Rangers team for 25 years. They had the likes of Ally McCoist and Trevor Steven, and to finish second to them was not a bad effort in a way, and we beat them in an Old Firm game, with me getting the winner.

Brady was a great motivator, and he showed that, by putting me in the starting line-up straight away, he was effectively saying: "I've put you in because I think you should be in that team." In a situation like that, you know if you have got any self-doubts you've got to lose them pretty quickly, and in my second game I scored the winning goal, so I justified his decision.

At Middlesbrough, because I was injured a lot, I got a bit down in the dumps and started doubting myself; but scoring in my second game at Celtic really helped, and so did the crowd's reaction, because they were chanting my name. All of a sudden you are thinking, "I want a bit more of this", and I was young and hungry and I wanted to carry on scoring.

I ended up as sub quite a lot because Charlie Nicholas played his way back into the team, but I finished top scorer with 15 goals in my first season, and I ended up with 20 in 36 games overall, which was a good record, especially because I was sub in 15 of those games.

Charlie Nicholas, who of course is a Sky pundit now, was a bit peeved when he was dropped for me, like anyone would be if they were dropped, but he was OK with me about it. I was the whipping boy at the time over that running track incident and he had a good laugh at me when I did that, but he was a good guy and I always got on with him.

And believe me, he was a brilliant player, absolutely brilliant. You know how good ex-Burnley ace Robbie Blake is with two feet and turning people inside out? Well, Charlie was better. He scored one of the best goals I've ever seen, watching the ball come over his head and catching it with his right foot. He also got two for Arsenal in their 1987 League Cup Final win over Liverpool, so he was a legend anyway.

I always got on with Charlie and he was a great guy, but even he didn't compare with Frank McAvennie, who was such a happy-go-lucky, funny guy, who was always bouncing around.

You have got to picture the scenario. When I was first at Celtic I was in a hotel and Frank McAvennie was in the next room to me. I didn't know Frank, but knew he played for West Ham, had blond hair and was always in magazines and the tabloids. At the time, he was going with a Page 3 girl called Jenny Blythe, and he was being seen at pop concerts and had done this and done that.

His girlfriend was living in London, so one midweek night when we had the following day off, Frank asked me if I wanted to go out for a few beers. Now Liam Brady had pulled me and warned me not to go out with Frank, but I was on my own in the hotel, so I was up for it.

The two of us and Joe Miller, who was a classy right winger, went out, but it was just the Frank Show really. He was the most popular bloke in Scotland with the birds because he was funny and good looking and anyone who'd been in the showers with him knew he had the biggest knob in Scotland. He could pull any bird he wanted and everyone loved him everywhere we went.

Now obviously, Frank had one or two problems at the time which I didn't know about and we don't need to go into, but I will say he kept going to the toilet on a regular basis and I didn't realise why, and I also found I was getting paralytic and he wasn't, so I knew there could have been something going on!

We would go to a place called the Piano Bar, which was upstairs at a nice club called Victoria's in Glasgow. Ally

McCoist and Mark Hateley went there, with all their designer gear, i.e. waistcoats costing three and a half grand and the like. To put it bluntly, there was fanny everywhere, top class stuff, though some of them might have been hookers for all I knew. Frank had one on each arm and models hanging around him, and he was living the playboy lifestyle to the full.

Champagne Charlie was Charlie Nicholas's nickname, but you can't blame him because everything was free. The bar owners gave you drinks free because they wanted the fans to know Celtic players drank there so it would be good for business.

Anyway, on this night, we'd been to a night club and, while I wasn't paralytic because I wasn't a massive drinker, Frank had been downing these drinks called Long Vodkas like a fish. We ended up going back to the hotel and Frank had a load of birds with him, but the bloke on the door says, "No problem, Frank", and we got drinks in the foyer at four in the morning. I had to go to bed because I was drunk now, but they were all still up and I don't know what they got up to.

But Liam Brady had his spies out and got to hear about it and he pulled me and said: "I've told you I don't want you going out with McAvennie", and I got a real bollocking for it and was warned off him big style. As for Frank, he could have got away with murder, but at the end of the day, he got 13 goals that season, so he did well.

Many of the players at the time seemed to have married their childhood sweethearts and were happy enough and so they didn't want to go to nightclubs, and though us younger lads did want to, we knew which was the right way and which was the wrong way to go about it, and if you played it the right way it was a fantastic lifestyle.

It really was a pressure way of life if you played for the Old Firm. You've got your Celtic pubs, where there is a poster on every wall and the whole pub has green and white scarves everywhere. If you go in there you are a hero, especially if you scored against Rangers, as I did.

However, I didn't go out that much because we were told to be careful and certainly after an Old Firm game not to go out because you don't know who is Celtic and who is Rangers and whether they are going to pat you on the back or hit you over the head with a bottle. That's how bad it could be.

In the Celtic areas, pubs were all green and white and then you would have your Rangers pubs which were all red, white and blue, and they fucking hated each other. If I had walked into a Rangers pub I am certain I would have got annihilated because somebody would have probably thought it was something to do with me taking the piss religion-wise or something like that, I guess.

Glasgow was generally very scary and my hotel room on the 2nd floor overlooked the bus station and the red-light area, and you could see all the prostitutes pulling old blokes, even 90-year-olds. Sometimes, if I walked to the shop near the hotel, the pros would approach you and say, "Are you looking for it?"

But the fact that I'd started scoring straight away when I signed for Celtic meant I always got a really good reaction when I went out, though maybe if I had done nothing it might have been different.

Most people think there are only two teams in Scotland and obviously you've got the two massive Glasgow giants, Rangers and Celtic, but there are other clubs.

When you go to Aberdeen, they have a good ground and it's always a hard game, as is Dundee United away and Motherwell away. If you play for the Old Firm, you are expected to win and you are odds-on at the bookies, so there is a lot of pressure. But the Aberdeens and Dundee United's of this world have European experience and are tough sides to play, and even St Johnstone, whose McDiarmid Park was a mini-version of Ibrox, was a good ground and a tough place to go.

What I found was that the pressure you were under when you were expected to win every single game was intense, and you knew even the Old Firm would slip up sometimes, as Celtic did at Inverness at the end of last season.

There were, of course, some really crappy grounds as well. One was Stenhousemuir's Ochilview Park. We played them in the Scottish Cup and won 9-0 and I got a hat-trick, but Frank McAvennie got a hat-trick too and he claimed the match ball because he said he got his first. But the thing was, there was still pressure on you to win, even at those types of grounds.

There was always the religious divide everywhere too, and even, say, Aberdeen fans would be either Catholic or Protestant and therefore Celtic or Rangers, and the intensity up there was unbelievable. People hated each other to a point where they would threaten to kill them, as has been proved recently with the Neil Lennon incidents.

Just the fact that I played for Celtic meant I was often

the subject of vitriolic songs, and many fans would call me a Catholic bastard and hate me with a passion just because I put green and white on.

Funnily enough, the Rangers and Celtic players got on OK.

Ally McCoist was a great guy and a funny lad, and he had a brilliant goalscoring record up there. He was nice as pie and always said, "All right, Andy. How's its going?" when he saw me. Mark Hateley was OK, but he was a bit stuck-up. He was about 6ft 5ins and dripping in jewellery, and was always covered in really expensive designer gear.

And it was unbelievable seeing Trevor Steven again. As a 15-year-old kid, I remember getting his autograph down at Burnley's Gawthorpe training ground. He was a great player for the Clarets and I stood at the gates at Gawthorpe and waited for him to sign, which was shortly before I was released by Burnley.

And now, seven years later, I'm walking out in front of 60,000 people and he's playing for Rangers and I'm playing for Celtic. I was already top scorer on 14 in 20 games, but I scored the winner. Part of me felt like saying: "I've got your autograph. Do you not remember me?" It's a small world and the odds on that kid asking for Steven's autograph going on to score the winner against a team he was playing for must have been eight billion to one.

All in all, I was very proud to play for Celtic.

I had some good times at Celtic and, particularly in the early days, things went well.

At the end of my first season, we finished second in the league to a very good Rangers team which included the likes of Ally McCoist and Trevor Steven. And from a personal angle, I was top scorer with 15 goals, one more than Gerry Creaney, but I'd only played about 23 games, so was quite happy.

But we were beaten 1-0 in a Scottish Cup semi-final against Aberdeen at Hampden Park. The Dons were a decent side, with the excellent Eoin Jess up front, but we dominated the game and it was a disaster to lose it.

And though Rangers were a good side, Liam Brady was coming under increasing pressure, because finishing second to Rangers is not good enough up there, such is the pressure.

At the end of the season, we had about a month off, so I came back down to Burnley, then went to see my son Charley in Hull for a while.

About that time, I was wondering about international call-ups. A lot of Scottish players I played with had been capped by Scotland and if I was Scottish, I'm sure I would have got a cap, because I was better than a lot of them; but I didn't get capped by England, though I was told I was near to being selected for England B on one occasion. I always wondered how I would have responded because at every level I played at I always finished top scorer. I felt confident enough to think I'd do all right.

When I was a kid and I was banging in goals for Hull, I was looking at the players that were getting in the under-21's squad at the time and thinking, "Well, I should have a chance", but I think, because Hull were a bit unfashionable, it went against me. I was the subject of a big write-up once which said Trevor Cherry, the ex-Leeds player who was

England B manager at the time, had been to watch me a few times, but I never actually got called up. I think if I had been at Leeds I would have got in, but you have got to believe in yourself and I kept doing that.

Anyway, before I knew it, I was back in pre-season training and then we went on a pre-season tour to Italy. Liam Brady was obviously a legend over there, as he had played so well in the Italian League and was very popular; but while we were on tour, the sad news about Tommy Coyne's wife came in, and, following as it did the news of Tony Mowbray's wife, there was something of a sombre atmosphere.

We were based up in the mountains because it was the middle of summer and it was cooler up there, and one day we played Lazio, who were based near us, and we were beaten 1-0 in a game played behind closed doors; but mostly it was just hard training.

We trained the Italian way over there. That meant we got up in the morning and had breakfast at about 7.30am, then trained from 9am till 11am, before going back to the hotel, which was more like a hostel as we were sleeping in these large rooms with five of us in each one. We'd have a break for an hour and have something to eat, then go back training from noon till about 2.30pm, go back and rest again and then start training again at 5pm till about 7ish, when we'd have a meal all together then go to bed. You were absolutely shattered because you were doing three hard sessions a day for about a week.

It was hard, but it was great to experience another side of football and it was the kind of thing some players never get to experience, so it was great for my development as a player.

When we got back to Glasgow, we had a good start to the new season and I had a good start personally, scoring five goals in the first four games, a couple of them after coming off the bench.

But Brady was coming under increasing pressure and ex-Celtic player Lou Macari's name kept being bandied about in the press as a replacement, and all of a sudden, at the end of September, Brady got the sack.

It wasn't a great shock because of all the speculation, but when a manager who has signed you leaves the club, you obviously wonder what the future holds.

Most of the players respected Brady but, as is always the case, those who he played respected him more, while those not in the team were probably glad to see the back of him. Stuart Slater was probably happy enough, because at least he could now get out. The lad's confidence had gone completely and he was relieved to get a move to Ipswich.

When Lou Macari took over, we were all hoping to get picked, but we played a European game in Portugal and there was a rule about a maximum of four foreign players in the team. As I was English, I was classed as foreign, so travelled over but missed out on the team, which was bad news.

After we flew home, the lads who didn't play were told to meet at the club at 1pm. The training ground had a running track round it and Macari said: "Right, lads. We are going to do some running."

We all looked at each other, thinking: "Oh, fucking hell. He is going to run the bollocks off us." The players who had been under him in the past had said he would just run you stupid as he was into 10-mile runs and all sorts of ridiculous things.

Macari said: "Right, we are going to time you and if you can do two laps in 120 seconds, you can go home. But if you don't do it in that time, we are going to carry on."

We all looked at each other again and I was thinking: "Well, I am going for this anyway.""

But really what he had asked us to do was virtually impossible unless you were a trained athlete. I did the first lap in about 58 seconds and the second lap in about 64, so had to carry on, but you would have absolutely killed yourself in trying to beat the time. He knew what he was doing and he was laughing while he was doing it.

It was a nightmare and we all knew then it was going to be hard under Macari, and pretty soon a couple of senior players such as Charlie Nicholas made it clear they didn't like him.

To be honest, he wasn't with us that much because his assistant, Ashley Grimes, who used to be at Manchester United with him, was with us a lot of the time and he also brought his own fitness coach.

I wasn't impressed with him because he played a long-ball style, and also because he wouldn't play me, even though I was scoring in every single game for the reserves and really looking sharp. I wanted first-team football because I had already tasted it, so I wasn't happy.

Chapter 5 Back Down To Earth

What happened next was incredible. I thought Hull and Burnley were interested, but it was actually Barnsley who came in for me and their manager was Viv Anderson, who was of course one of England's first ever black players. I went in a swap deal, with Wayne Biggins, who had a spell at Burnley, going the other way.

Now, in my opinion, Biggins couldn't lace my boots goal-scoring wise, and the proof of the pudding is that when he went to Celtic he never scored a single goal for them. That to me said everything. I was a bit surprised, but Macari had had him before at Stoke and some managers take players with them who they think can cut it.

Liam Brady was the same with Stuart Slater, who was a great lad who I got on with. But Stuart buckled under the pressure and couldn't buy a goal, even though Liam played him in every single position along the forward line. But he stuck by him because he was his record signing at £1.8million, which at the time was a lot of money.

Brady just kept sticking with Stuart and then, when he left the club, Macari made it clear early doors that I wasn't in his plans. He didn□t say anything, but it was obvious because I was not involved in the squad.

He had one eye on Biggins and must have spoken about a swap deal, and Stan Ternent sort of acted as my agent when we went for talks with Viv Anderson and Danny Wilson at Barnsley. They had to work hard to sell the club to me because, though they were re-developing the ground at the time and had one massive stand which was up and looked OK, the rest of the ground was not that clever.

Macari said I could have first-team football and was basically offering me a way out, which still surprised me a bit because my record had been really good at Celtic and I still thought I might get a chance.

But at the age of 25 or 26, you don't want reserve-team football, so I left. Amazingly, I have never been back to Celtic Park to this day. The nearest had been bumping into former Celtic players such as Gerry Creaney, who I met when Barnsley played Portsmouth.

I remember looking at the Division One table and thinking Barnsley were doing OK, even though they were actually struggling a bit. So I rang Stan Ternent and explained that I didn't have an agent because the contract I had with Eddie Gray had finished, and Stan came across independently to advise me.

We had talks with Viv Anderson and Danny Wilson, who were great guys, and they told me I was going to play in the first team straight away. I looked at the Barnsley team and they were a good set of lads, and I looked at the location, which was not far from my family, and although it was hard leaving a big club, harder in fact than I realised at the time, I signed immediately and was training with them the next day.

Barnsley thought they had got a bit of a coup because of the fact that I had scored so many goals for Celtic and they had tied things up so quickly, and in hindsight I probably jumped the gun and I could have gone to a bigger club, and that is no disrespect to Barnsley.

I actually took a pay cut because I got a £30,000 signing-on fee and a £750-a-week two-and-a-half-year deal. But they were a great set of lads and they had some good players, such as Andy Rammell, Gerry Taggart, Owen Archdeacon, Neil Redfearn, Brendan O'Connell and Darren Sheridan.

We did well, but I found Barnsley a bit of a dour place and the difference between playing there and at Celtic was massive. I thought: "Christ, you had everything on a plate at Celtic." You were looked after, you would go up to the restaurant after training and get anything, while there was a working men's club at the end of the stand at Barnsley and it was like a scene from the film Kes. Everybody obviously had that Barnsley twang, women included obviously, and it was hard work adjusting.

I played up front with Andy Liddell and with a young lad called Chris Jackson, who broke into the England under-18 squad and who looked a real prospect. I played up front with him on my debut and he scored, while I had to wait until my second game for my first goal.

Sadly, Chris suffered severe head injuries in a car crash later that season. It was yet another case of a tragedy hitting a playing colleague. He ended up in a wheelchair and it was really upsetting when we went to see him, because he had been such a great prospect.

We were struggling in the league by then, but I started scoring and I think I ended up with 13 goals in about 25 games and we stayed up quite comfortably. But crowds were mediocre, averaging about eight or nine thousand, while for a big derby against someone like Sheffield United there might be about 15,000, and to be honest the facilities were crap.

Viv Anderson was great, but about two months after I joined, Bryan Robson took over at Middlesbrough and took Viv with him. Barnsley were really penny-pinching at the time and they had no money, and it was such a contrast to flying around Europe with Celtic. And eventually, almost as a cost-cutting measure, they gave the job to Danny Wilson, who became player-manager.

Viv Anderson and Danny Wilson were similar, but I must admit I think Viv knew he was leaving Barnsley.

I guess that was partly because they weren't really a big club, but more because the Barnsley fans were so dour it was beyond belief. For example, we were sixth in what would today be the Championship and we were being booed off by our own fans. There would be 40 blokes watching us train every morning and the attitude was just so downbeat. I know a lot of people were struggling on the dole at the time, but Barnsley in those days was a really depressing place and it was a real doom-and-gloom scenario.

I just got the feeling Viv had had enough and I got the impression straight away that he knew he wasn't going to be there long, even though he had just signed me. But he was a great guy and a really upbeat fellow and I took to him straight away.

Danny Wilson was very much in the Viv Anderson mould:

easy going and laid back, but a very, very good coach. He wasn't into the bollockings and shoutings thing and he would get his point across a bit more constructively.

I remember a training session after Viv had left for Middlesbrough. It was a Friday, which was always a bit of a chore getting into Barnsley. There would be Steve Davis, Darren Sheridan and myself and we would always get stuck on the M62, even though we set off at about 7.30 in the morning. After living at my parents' house for a while, I had this flat in Padiham and I'd set off and pick up Darren Sheridan in Bury because he couldn't drive. This particular Friday morning, we had a real struggle with the traffic and got to the training ground about five or 10 minutes late, which usually meant we'd get a fine.

But Danny got all the lads over and he said: "Right, go home if you want."

Everyone looked at each other and said: "What?"

"You can go home if you want, but I want three points tomorrow," he said, and that was that. So we did, and surprise, surprise, we won the day after.

He tried loads of things to keep up the team spirit; for instance, if we had a night out, he'd insist on everyone going and it became a bonding thing.

But he was a great guy and a great manager. Swindon, where he was previously, have had a bad time recently, but he did well for them generally and I'm not surprised, because he was a good manager and a very, very good motivator. He led by example because Danny was still playing at the time and he was so fit. He had to be to keep up with some really fit lads at Barnsley such as Neil Redfearn and Andy Liddell, who really looked after themselves and if you didn't follow suit in training you were left behind.

Danny's assistant was Eric Winstanley, who had been at Barnsley his entire career. I think he was one of those players like Brian Miller at Burnley who'd been there from a schoolboy and risen through the ranks. He was a big centre half and he looked like the TV detective Magnum, because he had a big tash and he was 6ft 3ins. He was 50-plus by then, but he had been a hard man in his time. He was a really good guy, but he still had that hard streak.

I remember one incident on the training ground when Eric had taken the under-18s and he had them all in a circle in front of him while he was giving a team talk. Danny Wilson had called me over and we were about 20 yards away talking. I had my back to Eric and then a ball just happened to roll towards me, so I turned and just kicked it. I turned back to the manager and, as I was talking, I saw his face change, because when I kicked the ball it had hit Eric right on the side of the head. Danny started laughing and just said under his breath: "You'd better get running, because you've just hit Eric in the face in front of the under-18s."

I turned round and looked and Eric said: "Are you fucking taking the piss?"

I said, "I'm sorry, Eric", but he chased me round the training ground for about 30 seconds till he got out of breath. It was a complete accident, but I hit him plumb on the side of his face while he was giving his team talk and I think I knocked his false teeth out. I thought he was going to kill me and it took him about two hours to calm down. It was a classic.

Eric was Barnsley through and through and while Danny could give a bollocking, Eric was a master at it. He would let you know in no uncertain terms if he thought you were shirking or getting the run-around or whatever.

Eric was really aggressive but also a good guy, and he went on to manage Barnsley after I had left. He then went on to coach the St Kitts and Nevis team in the Caribbean, and I heard he apparently left his wife and married one of the natives.

Darren Sheridan, who we called 'Sheds', ended up becoming my best mate at Barnsley because we used to travel in every day. Sheds had come from non-league and some weeks he'd be out on a Sunday because we knew on a Monday he'd do absolutely nothing in training.

I knew Steve Davis, who had been at Burnley, and even though he'd been injured for ages, he was unbelievably dedicated. There were so many times Sheds and I were on the motorway and we'd be saying to him, "Look, just ring in and say you have had a puncture and we'll go in those services now and get a full English and just go home", but he never would.

There was one particular time when we had a tough home midweek game and I went to pick Sheds up at Bury bus station. I was waiting and waiting and eventually had to set off, because we had to be at the ground by 6.30pm. There were hardly any mobile phones then, and though I had one the size of a suitcase, Sheds didn't, so that was that.

When I got to the ground, the boss said: "Where's Sheds?"

I said, "I haven't got a clue"; but apparently I'd missed him by about two seconds. I wasn't to know, because I had been waiting ages, but I remember him just bursting into the dressing room at about five minutes to seven calling me a bastard and saying I'd left him. We all started laughing, because he'd rung Danny up and told him he was on his way, and he was in time to play and did well.

Sheds was a great lad and a really good character and he is still in football now. He is probably one of the funniest lads I've ever come across. He would always have a joke ready. He was also very, very under-rated; I always thought he was a really good player.

He had six brothers, the most famous being John, of course, and they were a really rum family with some real characters who were always getting in trouble, but had their heart in the right place. Sheds would do anything for you, except buy a round of drinks; he was just a great lad all round.

When I was at Barnsley, Danny Wilson played three up front and I played with three really good strikers.

There was Andy Rammell, who was an ex-Manchester United trainee, who was about 6ft 2ins and very muscular, so was really good in the air and really good to play off. He scored his fair share of goals as well and I had a good partnership with him.

But we also had the up-and-coming Andy Liddell, who went on to break Wigan's goal-scoring record and had a really good career. He was also a really good goal-scorer and 'Lidds', as we called him, was basically trying to get my place in the team. He put me under pressure, but that was good really because I had some healthy competition. Lidds reminded me a bit of myself really, because he was young and cocky and believed in himself, as you have to if you want to be a good player.

We also had a lad called Chris Jackson, who was an under-19 international, plus another ex-Burnley player in Brendan O'Connell. Brendan was a striker at Turf Moor and was top scorer with 14 goals one season, but at Barnsley he played in midfield. What Brendan would do was gamble on Andy Rammell's flick-ons, and he got really good at timing his runs and scored a lot of important goals for Barnsley in that role, just playing behind the front two. He was really effective for Barnsley and I got on great with Brendan. He was a good lad, a good player and one of the funny guys in the team and a real joker in the dressing room.

I scored the 100th goal of my career when I was at Barnsley. It was actually a tap-in against Watford. Somebody hit the underside of the bar and I knocked it in and went on to score a hat-trick in an easy win.

By coincidence, I think my best goal for Barnsley was in

the same game. I was always predominately right-footed and, though I worked hard on my left foot throughout my career, it became like the old swinger, as they call it. But on this occasion, we had a throw-in on the right and I let it come over my shoulder and turned and hit it first time with my left foot from probably about 35 yards out. It came down right in the postage stamp gap in the corner. It really stuck out as being my best-ever goal.

At Barnsley, we didn't have what you'd call a team of stars, but if you went through the team we had some great players.

Danny was a brilliant manager and I would get on with him if I bumped into him tomorrow. He wasn't a bollocker and you weren't in fear of him, but he got on great with the players and he was a really good motivator who also led by example because he was still really fit.

There were some real characters in the team at Barnsley. I'd only been there a couple of months and the club's Christmas do came up. Darren Sheridan lived in Manchester and I was picking him up every day in Bury and driving him to training. The Christmas do was fancy dress, so I went to a place in Accrington and got a Batman costume and he'd gone as Robin. Sure enough, we broke down on the motorway after I had a puncture, so we got picked up and taken into Kwik-Fit in Bury dressed as Batman and Robin. They were all taking the piss out of us, but we got over to Barnsley in the end.

Lee Buckley, a good keeper who had played for Villa, was

another big character. On the same night, we had all met up at this pub where they were having a lock-in and he was dressed as a copper. He went out and stood in the middle of the road and put his hand up and apparently caused a pile-up.

Then Brendan O'Connell, who had played for Burnley, told me there were strippers on who really went for it, and I'm telling you, he was right. Brendan said if we wanted to have a go at the strippers, we could do. I couldn't believe what he was saying, but a few of the lads did and got on with it. I didn't have anything to do with it, but to be honest I was shocked. I had never seen owt like that before, but I suppose it was good for team spirit!

As I said, there were some great characters there such as Gerry Taggart, Andy Liddell, who was a very good player and went on to do very well for Wigan, and Nicky Eadon, who went to Birmingham for big money.

They were all welcoming at Barnsley, but you have always got to prove yourself and you know you cannot be giving it the 'Big Time Charlie' stuff, especially because facilities were so basic. We had a kit man called Norman Rimmington, whose nickname was Rim, and he'd been there about 100 years. He was Barnsley through and through and always having a crack with the lads. He was a great guy, but another one who was like a character from Kes.

Barnsley was a mining area, but virtually all the pits had shut down, so you would get a lot of fans coming to watch us train because they had lost their jobs. I had every sympathy for them, but to be honest they were such dour bastards.

There would be about 40 of them and you knew if we had got beaten on a Saturday or if you'd had a bad game, there would just be complete silence as you were walking past. It was horrible and they would be there every fucking day, and you might just about get a "well done" if you'd scored.

When I signed for Celtic, there was a packed press conference, but when I got to Barnsley there was just the local reporter there, so it was right back down to planet earth again.

Barnsley hadn't really done anything for years, but I left the club and went to Huddersfield, and the following season they got promoted to the Premier League with the same set of players. I felt that as though I had put so much work in and was so frustrated to then not be a part of it, but it was my choice to go to Huddersfield. They offered me £500 a week more, so it was an easy decision.

But the lads were fantastic and the manager was fantastic. It was just that the actual club and the place itself were really dour.

I scored 20 goals for Huddersfield that season and we challenged for a while, but we faded away at the end and Barnsley kept winning. I remember we played Southend away in the last game and listened on the radio as Barnsley got promoted. I couldn□t believe all the players that I'd been playing with were up to the Premier League.

I had the option to stay and they wanted me to stay, but I couldn't do it because of the money Huddersfield offered me.

We ended up finishing about mid-table in my first season at Barnsley and I ended up top scorer. I had a big rivalry with Neil Redfearn for the top scorer spot, but Neil had had a head start on me. I was one behind when we played Bolton in our last away game. We beat them 3-1 and I got two and overtook him, so he was not happy, especially after an incident in the previous game against Portsmouth.

We were going down on the bus and Owen Archdeacon, the regular penalty taker, was injured, so the manager said: "Right, who's on penalties?" Myself and Readfearn both said, "I'll take it", and neither of us were budging, so Danny Wilson, who you remember was player-manager at the time, said to me: "Right, if I get brought down, I'll take it, but otherwise you can have it."

Anyway, we were getting beaten 2-0 in the last minute and I was clean through and the centre-half hacked me down and it was a clear penalty. I got up and turned round and Redfearn had the ball on the penalty spot, so I said, "Give me the fucking ball", and he went, "Fuck off".

I said: "Give me the fucking ball."

"Are you fucking captain?" he said, and I reminded him what had happened on the coach.

The bottom line is that he wouldn't give me the ball and we were going to end up having a fight, so he took it and scored. I was disgusted because obviously I wanted to score and I had already sorted out that I was taking the penalties, and as he ran past me after he'd scored, he gave me a little tap just to rub it in.

But I had the last laugh with those two goals at Bolton in the last game and I remember saying in the dressing room that at least I finished top scorer, and he just stormed off.

Neil was a good lad, but he always wanted to be top scorer. He'd always get 15 goals from midfield and he was a really good player and did well out of a few moves at the latter end of his career, which was fine because he looked after himself and stayed fit.

I got one over on him that day though and he didn't like it, and the following season I got 20 and he got about 15, but he was always second top scorer which, for a midfielder, was brilliant. He was always into double figures and he'd score some absolute screamers.

We had one or two good cup clashes when I was at Barnsley, including a home tie against Arsenal when I was up against Tony Adams and Martin Keown at the centre of their defence and they had Ian Wright up front. They beat us 3-0, but what I remember is the way they played such a tight offside game: I was caught as soon as I moved and had no space. I had to drop back and our midfield was getting in the way because they were stifling us so well. We didn't create anything.

Keown and Adams were unbelievably aggressive and big and strong and absolutely kicked the shit out of you. You'd turn into elbows all the time and though it wasn't that long ago, you wouldn't get away with it now.

I remember Keown having a go at me. He came through me and then told me to get up, or something like that. I ended up telling him to fuck off, but that was it. They were a good side, you had to respect that.

I enjoyed my time at Barnsley, but I had to go when Huddersfield came in for me. Danny Wilson was a great manager and a great guy, and there was a great team spirit and we had some really good times. But after getting 47 goals for them in two-and-a-half seasons, my contract was up and they offered me a grand a week rather than £750, so I went to Huddersfield.

Now, we'd knocked Huddersfield out of the cup and I had scored a hattrick and I remember seeing Brian Horton, who was Terriers boss at the time, in a car park, and he persuaded me to move there.

Chapter 6 Back With Horton

Barnsley were playing Oldham away right near the end of the season when my contract was up and, as sometimes can happen at Oldham, the fog came down from Saddleworth Moor. All the crowd were in and it was only a few minutes before kick-off, but the fog set in and they had to call the game off. It lifted about 30 minutes later, but at the time you couldn't see; it was a real pea-souper.

I'd driven myself because I was living over here and I was going back to the car when I heard somebody shouting my name, so I looked round and it was Horton. I'd scored a hat-trick against his team about three months earlier. We were 2-0 down from the first leg at Huddersfield, but we beat them 4-0 in the home leg and I scored the hat-trick. He must have been impressed and basically it was a form of poaching, let's be honest about it.

He shouted me over and asked how I was doing and asked when my contract was up. I told him it was up now, because it was almost the end of season, and he said: "Do you fancy coming playing for me at Huddersfield? We are going to sign a few players and get things moving."

He took my phone number and then rang me up a couple of days later and told me they hadn't agreed a fee or anything but that if I wanted to come he wanted me to sign. He said he was signing Marcus Stewart for big money and he wanted me to play up front with him.

Marcus was younger than me but a good player and went on to do really well for Ipswich in the Premier League; and myself, Marcus and Andy Morrison, a big lad who had been centre-half at Blackburn, all signed on the same day.

Horton had sort of marked my card that day and when I realised that I was going to be offered more money, I knew I had to go. I had no agent at the time and just used the PFA because Stan Ternent had by then got the Bury job, so I couldn't officially get in touch with him. However, Ronnie Jepson, who was at Huddersfield at the time, knew Stan, so we could get round that.

I went for talks at Huddersfield's ground, which was then called the McAlpine Stadium, and I remember thinking the stadium looked quite futuristic at the time and I thought they were going places. It was also a bit nearer my family and friends.

Huddersfield had just got promoted to what is now the Championship and so were in the same division as Barnsley at the time, but they looked like they had a better vision for the future. They had signed a few players and just looked a better set-up. In addition, I had been at Barnsley two and a half years and I wanted a change.

Brian Horton was manager, and Dennis Booth, who had also been at Hull when I was there, was coach, so it was like going back to Hull - but a better set-up. We started off quite well and myself and Marcus were both scoring, and by Christmas we were in the top six and looking good.

It was not all great though. I can remember the big derby game when Huddersfield played Bradford City and this particular game was televised live on Sky, so it was even more of a pressure match. We were up against it because Bradford had a good side with players such as Chris Waddle in the line-up, but I was doing well and was already in double figures for the season by this time.

Unfortunately, we had a nightmare start when Waddle took a corner and our keeper, to be honest, completely cocked it up by missing the cross and we were one down. Within half an hour, we were 3-0 down and the Huddersfield fans were going mental. I think a few had thrown away their season tickets and they were booing and, when we went in at half-time three down, they were chanting "Horton out".

Brian Horton went absolutely berserk in the dressing room, chucking stuff around as he always did and shouting at us, "My job's on the fucking line", and things like that.

But after the break, we got it back to 3-1 and the fans had started getting on our side a little bit and then Marcus Stewart made it 3-2.

Marcus was the club's "Golden Bollocks", if you will, because he was the record signing and a great player. I had scored just as many goals though, and we had a really good partnership up front. He had scored something like 25 goals in a season at Bristol Rovers and had a similar record to the one I had at Hull. In one particular game away to Ipswich, we won 3-0 and I scored two with Marcus getting the other; we worked so well together that day.

We were combining really well, but then he picked up an

injury which kept him out for about three months. Basically, he was a really good player and I think if he had stayed fit, we could have made the play-offs. He ended up going to Ipswich and getting 20 goals in the Premier League, so he proved what a good player he was.

Back to that game at Bradford and we eventually made it 3-3 and then we were all over them looking for the winner. Then, in the last 30 seconds, I made a run and somebody put me in, and I found myself going straight through towards the centre of goal. Now, nine times out of 10, I would have scored, but I tried to put it in the right-hand corner and messed it up by miskicking the ball. I was absolutely gutted, because the whistle went straight away afterwards and it would certainly have been the winner.

But that's part of the deal in playing up front. You have got to take the ups with the downs, forget about the miss and not let it destroy you.

Horton was obviously glad we got a result, but I got a real bollocking afterwards. There was none of this "Unlucky, pal", but you have got to take it at times like that because when you get all the praise when you win so you have got to take the stick when it goes wrong. It's just one of those things.

Andy Morrison was at the club at the time and not only was he a big bloke but he was a real hard case and absolutely mental. He was so bad; I think he'd been on anger management courses a couple of times, but it didn't seem to do any good. Andy was always fighting in nightclubs and was always in trouble. I heard he once had an altercation with a bus driver in Huddersfield and ended up actually pulling over in front of the bus, getting out of his car and jumping up and trying to strangle the bus driver.

He was a big, solid bloke with a real evil streak and I was always trying to keep on the right side of him. He was at Blackburn, Plymouth and Manchester City, among other clubs, and was an animal, unbelievably aggressive; but he was also a very good player. Not many players liked playing against him because the first thing he would do before a game was to say: "I'm going to smash your fucking face in."

He signed from Blackpool on the same day as myself and Marcus joined Huddersfield. Andy had just been in trouble there because Blackpool had won 2-0 at Bradford in the first leg of the play-off semi-final to set up a Wembley trip and then threw it away by losing the second leg 3-0 at home. Andy had put a bet on Bradford to win 3-0 just to cover himself and when it came in, he made a few quid. Unfortunately, the press got hold of it and had a field day when they knew he was betting against his own team. He was lucky to get away with that one.

After Marcus got injured, I was mostly playing on my own up front. I still managed 19 goals in the season, but we had a bad run and at one stage went nine games without a win.

At the time, Huddersfield had just moved to their new ground, which at that time was called the McAlpine Stadium. It had a futuristic design for that period and I think people in Huddersfield thought, because of it, they deserved to be in the Premier League, but they had only just gained promotion from the third tier and weren't exactly a massive club.

That winless run included a 6-0 thrashing in a midweek

game at Swindon Town. I wasn't playing as I had a hamstring injury, but I remember watching Teletext and seeing goal after goal going in and thinking: "Fucking hell." I knew the manager was under severe pressure and you just knew what was going to happen.

It's cruel to say, but when you are not playing, you don't want the team to win and the man whose playing in your position to get five goals. It's harsh, but at the end of the day, you want to be in the squad and so there is always part of you which wants the team to lose. Any player who denies that is bullshitting.

Brian Horton actually survived that season, but we had a bad start to the beginning of the next season and that finished him off; it seemed the board wanted him out anyway because they wanted a change.

Probably about three months before I signed for Huddersfield, I had scored a hat-trick against them for Barnsley and knocked them out of the League Cup. I definitely never thought anything of it at first, but as time went on, it became obvious to me that some Huddersfield fans never really forgave me. I'm not saying the fans didn't like me, but I think we milked it a bit and gave their fans some stick because we had been 2-0 down from the first leg, and it was never forgotten by some Terriers fans.

I wasn't that bothered anyway because, at the end of the day, I'm not from Huddersfield and had no deep affinity to the club. However, I was irritated that, though Marcus Stewart was a good player, he couldn't do any wrong in the fans' eyes, while I was getting called lazy and taking comments such as, "All he does is score". And that was after I'd scored 19 goals in a struggling side, which was a decent return, while Marcus, even though, to be fair, he had been injured, had only scored 11.

I stayed on at Huddersfield and remember scoring at Wrexham's Racecourse Ground, which was always a lucky one for me because I played there twice and scored both times. The first time I went there, I thought it would be hard because Wrexham as a club have a lot of history and tradition, even though I could see the ground had seen better days and the club now had no money. It was a really small crowd and all the pressure was on us because we were expected to win, and I got a goal in a hard-fought win and then eventually went back with Burnley and got my 200th career goal.

The Greek goalkeeper Nick Michopoulos, who everyone called 'Nick the Greek', came to Huddersfield on trial and didn't really perform, so didn't get a contract, but little did I know, some time later we'd meet up at Burnley.

But then Marcus picked up a bad injury which put him out for a few months and we never really replaced him. I carried on scoring, but we slipped down and finished mid-table.

I was there one season and finished top scorer and enjoyed it, but the following season, after starting well in pre-season, I picked up a hernia problem which started off as a niggle and got progressively worse. I started the first league game at home to Bradford and I scored, but I was in agony at the end of the game, and I had to have a hernia operation.

It was only meant to keep me out for about five weeks, but I came back a bit too soon and aggravated it again, so had to have the same op again. I had to go down to Harley Street to have it done properly by a top surgeon called Gilmore. The injury is a common sports injury which is now known as Gilmore's Groin. He operated on me and I was out for four months; but in that time Horton got the sack. He had been under a bit of pressure because he hadn't done as well as expected after Huddersfield had paid out quite a bit of money on players, and eventually the board had enough.

It was then that a previous incident came back to haunt me.

In that pre-season campaign before the injury struck, we had played a derby game against Halifax, who at the time were non-league. Playing for them at the back was Peter Jackson, who had been at Newcastle and Bradford, but was a bit of a legend at Huddersfield, where he had played for a long time. All the fans were singing his name and I was playing up front against him.

Then something happened after about half an hour, the like of which I have never experienced anywhere, despite playing at Celtic and a host of other clubs all over the place. Jackson just smacked me on the back of the head. I turned round and said: "What are you fucking doing?" Then he did it again, so I elbowed him in the face, as you would, because I couldn't believe he had done it.

As it was a friendly, the referee went over to the managers and said, "Can you take them both off, otherwise I am going to send them off", and the bosses obliged. We both got a bit of a bollocking from our respective managers, but I was angry because he was being disrespectful. He did it just to get a reaction.

The whole incident was largely forgotten about until during that long, boring period when I was going back to Huddersfield every day for treatment for that hernia, but still couldn't join the other players in training. Luckily in my career I didn't have that many injuries, but I can tell you it is crap, because you have to be in at 9am for treatment and back at 11am and 3pm.

But one day during that spell was much worse. Horton had been sacked and nobody knew who was going to get the job, but there were a lot of names being bandied about. All the lads got together and we were called to a meeting, because we were going to find out before the press who the new manager and assistant were.

We all sat in the dressing room and Terry Yorath, the ex-Leeds and Wales international, walked in, so then we wondered who would be his assistant. Would it be Dennis Booth, or it must be David Moss, who was at Luton with Horton and was a coach under him at Manchester City and left when Horton was sacked?

But the chairman then said Yorath was the assistant manager, and stood back to let in the new manager – and who walks in but Peter Jackson, who I had recently had that almighty clash with. "Fucking hell," I thought, unsurprisingly.

He'd been a player at Halifax and this was obviously his first managerial job.

I couldn't believe it, so I thought straight away that he was going to refer to the pre-season incident. The board probably thought that the crowd would be right back behind them because they all loved him.

Anyway, about two weeks later, I was fit again and went to see Jackson who, to his credit, said: "Forget about what happened in the pre-season game. That can happen to anyone. Don't worry about that. You are still in my plans."

I said: "No problem."

But the first reserve game I played after coming back from injury, Stan Ternent came to watch. I think Bury were doing a cheeky one and trying to sign me, but I wouldn't have gone there, even though Stan had done a brilliant job and got them up to the Championship.

Even though I'd trained hard, I didn't feel 100 per cent fit, as it was the first game back after a long lay-off. I didn't score and I remember I felt knackered and felt like I needed games.

But when I got home, the phone rang and it was Peter Jackson.

He said Burnley were coming in for me, and their manager Chris Waddle was going to ring me in a couple of minutes.

'Another goal for Barnsley' (Courtesy of Burnley Express)

'The last ever goal in the 90's in the football league'
(Courtesy of Burnley Express)

'The last ever player to score a hat-trick in the 90's this was against Oxford' (Courtesy of Burnley Express)

'Me with my Golden Boot a very proud moment in my career' (Courtesy of Michael Warn)

'We finished 2nd in the league to a very strong Rangers side, I finished Celtic's top scorer' (Courtesy of Lancashire Telegraph newspaper)

'I never wanted to leave but apparently I had no choice' (Courtesy of Burnley Express)

'I wanted to stay and play for Burnley no other club just Burnley, The last time I ever walked on the pitch at Turf Moor – Gutted!' (Courtesy of Burnley Express)

Back in football and loving it but his time as a manager and ironically tan's son is my assistant' (Courtesy f Burnley Express)

'Me and my 3 daughters, I'm a very proud father'
(Courtesy of Michael Warn)

Chapter 7 I'm Dreaming

When I initially signed for Burnley, I went down to the training ground in the middle of the night, parked up and just sat there in the car. Then I drove up to the new car park outside Turf Moor and just stared at the stands.

The Clarets were bottom of the league and, to be blunt, I was shitting myself. I really wanted to sign for them, but as it was the team I had supported all my life and which all my mates supported, I was that nervous that I might flop. I didn't know whether I was going to be successful, I didn't know whether I was going to score and I didn't know if I was going to get relegated.

They always say the hardest place to make it is in your own home town in front of your own fans, but I bit the bullet. I dropped a division, so I didn't need to sign, but I wanted to play for Burnley.

When I left Huddersfield, because I hadn't asked for a move I was entitled to a signing-on fee under the terms of my contract, and the money I was owed was £30,000 before tax, so it was no small figure.

But just as I was about to sign for Burnley, Huddersfield popped up and said: "Oh, you can go, but you can't have your signing-on fee though."

I always thought that they'd never appreciated me at Huddersfield and I remember being interviewed after a game and mentioning it.

I arrived back at the club I supported as a lad after a swap deal which involved Paul Barnes going in the opposite direction. He was a good striker who had got 24 goals for Burnley the previous season, so I knew when I came here I had to get more than that. Yet, not meaning any disrespect, I knew I was a better striker than him because I'd played for the likes of Celtic. Peter Jackson preferred him to me, so I always had a bee in my bonnet about that, but I was able to get my own back by getting that winning goal. I felt like shouting: "Have some of that, Huddersfield." It was a brilliant feeling.

Paul Barnes, by the way, had moved on by then and never hit the heights at Huddersfield, but for me it was fate to come back to Burnley. It's always great when you get your own back, and that day was fantastic because I celebrated in front of 3,000 travelling Clarets fans.

The keeper that day was Nic the Greek and I can remember Stan saying we are going to practice our finishing after training and Clarets boss Stan Ternent said: "Look, we've got this Greek on trial, so let's take the fucking piss out of him." I don't think Stan thought he was any good, but he put in probably the best performance I've ever seen. I was drilling balls in from everywhere and I thought I am going to score here and I'm going for it, but he had an unbelievable session and saved everything.

He was so good, he did enough to travel with the first

team on the Saturday, when by coincidence we were going to Huddersfield. Then regular keeper Paul Crichton was unbelievably unlucky, because he got stuck in traffic. Stan was going mental because, at the end of the day, it was Paul's responsibility to get there, and he had no option but to play Nic.

He probably had a bee in his bonnet because Huddersfield had released him, but whatever the reason, he had an absolutely unbelievable game and we won 1-0, with me getting the winner, which was fantastic because I was really getting my own back on my previous club.

Chris Waddle signed me for Burnley and, at the end of the day, I have a lot to thank him for. But we were in a desperate situation when he signed me. We were four points adrift at the bottom of the league and, with four clubs going down, I think I was the last throw of the dice for him.

Yet the move nearly didn't come about and wasn't straightforward by any means. What happened was, I agreed to go to Burnley and I went for talks, but Huddersfield still owed me my signing-on fee, which had been agreed when I joined them.

So, basically, what I had to say was, "Right, well I'm not signing then", and it was a case of calling each other's bluff. But I was absolutely certain I wasn't going to give in, because I'd earned that money and they were doing it just out of pure spite. I stuck to my guns and, although it delayed the move for probably about 10 days, I got the money and ended up signing.

I was still absolutely shitting myself and what made it

worse was that I wasn't match-fit because I'd had a double hernia and had only played one reserve game in four months.

As it happened, it all went OK. My home debut against Southend sticks in my mind because I was thinking: I just hope I don't feel absolutely shattered. I knew I had to be able to last 90 minutes because I didn't want the fans thinking: "What's the crack here? He's not fit."

I was knackered at the end, but I managed to keep going and I got the winning goal. Chris Waddle sent a ball down the overlap and then the ball was whipped in to the near post. I used to make that near post run a lot and though Richard Johnson, who was marking me, was a good player, I got in front of him and slammed it past Neville Southall for the only goal of the game.

I felt so proud and so relieved. I've got a good record with debuts with previous clubs, but this was 'the big one', as it was my home town team.

The first requirement is run your bollocks off and show the people that you care. I knew the Burnley fans would forgive Andy Cooke for anything because he did that and he was brilliant at it, and that's what fans pay their money for. He didn't get that many goals, but they forgave him because of his work rate. He just ran everywhere; I suppose Ian Moore also did that. I would say Cooke was a lot better, because he would get stuck in.

The fans want to see effort, but in that team there were a few players who didn't show that much. Burnley were bottom of the league in January and when you are there, it's for a reason, that you are the worst team in the league, and that's exactly what we were.

We had the likes of Mark Winstanley, who I didn't really like, and also Michael Williams, Steve Blatherwick and Mark Ford, and basically the team was getting beaten on a regular basis. They had no winners in the team and they got used to losing and they were plummeting big time.

But Gerry Harrison worked hard and did well, along with Paul Weller, Paul Smith and Andy Cooke, and, when I joined, we worked together to get us out of the shit.

And also I have got to say Chris Waddle was a key figure, because he played in every single one of those games late in the season. He didn't need to because he knew then he was going at the end of the season and he could have just 'tossed it off', so to speak, but he worked his bollocks off in those games and he was class; a really, really good player.

I still hear Burnley fans saying, "Fucking Chris Waddle, blah blah", but not only did he sign me for the club, which was great, but I saw how he worked his balls off on those last few games to keep us up. It was a miracle how he did it, because obviously with the players we had at the time we were just heading into the oblivion of the bottom division.

We were really struggling and then we had a run of fixtures against the likes of Grimsby, Northampton, Bristol City and Fulham, who were all near the top of the table. Fulham had just started spending money and had Chris Coleman and a few other big names, but we ended up beating them, even though, if you were a betting man, you'd never have given us a chance.

I'll be honest with you, in a couple of the games we got murdered really, and certainly didn't dominate every game, and we were hanging on in most of them; but fortunately I got the goal in each game and we picked up a few points. Bristol City in particular was one where I scored a pressure penalty and I was lucky enough to score it, and ended up with 13 goals that season in 19 appearances.

But there was an amazing incident when we were playing Walsall away. There had been a lot of speculation about other clubs being interested in keeper Marlon Beresford, but it all seemed normal when we were on the coach on our way to the game. A few of the lads were playing cards and some were watching a video when we pulled up at a services, where some of the players were due to get on, and Marlon gets off. We said, "Where's Marlon gone?", and were told he'd signed for Middlesbrough.

We were stunned. Chris Woods, who was the goalkeeping coach, had been a fantastic keeper in his time, but obviously he'd put weight on since then, but he ended up playing. We drew 0-0, but how we got a point I'll never know. We got battered, but held out, thanks to the grace of God.

But that's the predicament the club were in at that time, i.e. having to sell one of your main assets on the way to a game. Sell him on a Friday or during the week, but on the way to a game?

We stayed up with a last-day win over Plymouth, but Waddle was on his way, as we knew he was.

Chapter 8 Reunion With Stan

Whichever walk of life you're in, it's always a big moment when a new boss arrives.

When Waddle left Turf Moor that summer, there were a lot of names flying about with regard to who was going to get the job, and Stan Ternent was obviously mentioned. Stan had done a brilliant job at Bury and they were desperate to keep him. I remember them saying they weren't going to let him go, but Stan eventually got the job and I knew straight away that things were going to change.

The press had put it out that the Clarets had got their man because, though Bury had turned down the approach, I heard Stan just walked out on them and wanted everyone alerted to the fact that he loved Burnley. Sam Ellis came with him and I just knew straight away it would work because I knew Stan from Hull.

To be honest, under Waddle it was a piece of piss. We were having days off training and even when we were in, there was no running involved. We were really doing nothing and it was big cigars time.

But I knew just going off what I'd known of Stan in the past that it was going to be much tougher under him. He didn't mess about with people and he got results, and

I knew he would bring a load of players in, because he did that at Hull. Basically, you are always going to have competition at any club, so your place is always under threat, and that certainly proved to be the case for me, because he came in and brought in I don't know how many players. He completely changed the whole staff, and it got results.

I didn't get any special treatment, because he made it clear to everyone that they had to earn their place. I just knew every single day from then on was going to be intense, because there was none of this having days off; it was really hard work again.

Stan obviously knew it needed a complete overhaul. Nobody was safe, not even me, and we all knew it. I found out Stan was coming a few weeks before he arrived, so I put everything into getting fit before pre-season training started. I was flying, I had done so much running, but I did it on purpose because I knew what Stan was like, always testing people out and running them against each other.

He knew he had to get rid of a lot of the current squad. Even if you were under contract, it didn't matter. If that was the case, he'd get rid of you by just making you train on your own so you had no choice.

Stan knew he couldn't do it all at once, but he started bringing players in from Bury and we must have signed six players from Gigg Lane, though they were all better than what we had, to be fair.

He got rid of Blatherwick, Ford, Winstanley, Williams, a lad called Kevin Henderson, who played up front, and Paul

Smith; and Andy Cooke didn't last long with Stan either, even though the fans liked them.

Glen Little stayed, as did Paul Weller, though I think he became ill soon after; but Dean West came in, as did Gordon Armstrong, Lenny Johnrose, Peter Swan, Ronnie Jepson and the striker Tony Ellis.

Stan made Armstrong captain straight away. Now, at the end of the day, I'm Burnley through and through, while Gordon Armstrong's never played for Burnley in his life and doesn't give a toss about them really, so I felt he didn't really have any authority over me.

In one of the first games he was captain, he got the ball at centre-half and knocked it 30 yards over my head. It ran out of play, so I turned round and he was putting his arms up, so I said: "What are you fucking doing?"

He said, "You should get running after it", so I said, "Shut the fuck up", because I knew it was a terrible ball. He wouldn't admit it and was trying to blame me; so me and Armstrong didn't really get on from then onwards. There were a lot of players who came in and I knew it meant nothing to them to play for Burnley, and Armstrong was just 'Captain Yes Man' to Stan.

Dean West was OK, because he earned his place in the team. He got up and down the field and got crosses in and got stuck in, even though he was only little.

Ronnie Jepson only scored one goal for Burnley and didn't play that often because he couldn't really run by then; but he was a big, hard, aggressive bastard and he was great for the spirit in the dressing room. When he did come on, he'd rough people up and he'd say: "Right, I'm going to smash this cunt." The defenders were scared then and it was good for me because I got more chances.

Lenny Johnrose was, don't forget, ex-Blackburn, and I scored against him for Hull. I never got on with him because I was from Burnley and he was from Blackburn, and Lenny had a real attitude; but he was hard as nails and also one of the best at taking people out. Stan would say to him: "Right, Lenny. Sort fucking so-and-so out", and he would.

I ended up warming to him a little bit, but he was one of several players who would get jealous because I got the headlines, as I used to score all the time. The headlines in the papers would read, "Payton does it again", and they'd worked their bollocks off and never got a mention. If someone slagged me off in training or whatever, for a bit of banter I'd say, "Fuck off, I'm top scorer"; but Lenny and one or two others would hate that. So when I won the Golden Boot at the end of the season, I could ram it down their throats. I ended up getting 23 goals in Stan's first season at the club, which I was happy with, and we finished mid-table.

Yet Stan was still very touchy about the Bury connection. Ally Pickering, who had arrived from Stoke, made a joke one day in the dressing room about him not knowing the difference and Stan went absolutely mental for no reason. It was just a bit of a joke about the fact that every signing seemed to come via Bury. They were good players and Stan had done well there, getting them into the Championship, but I felt like they were taking over a little bit and became a bit of a clique.

Sometimes on a Sunday, players could go up to Stan's house for Sunday dinner, but I never did. I didn't mean any disrespect to Stan, but I wasn't into all that stuff.

I never went on the end-of-season holiday because, basically, I couldn't be arsed. At the end of a long season, the last thing I wanted to do was go on the piss for a week with all those lot, if you know what I mean. It became a bit of a standing joke, because Stan would say, Are you coming on the end-of-season golf day?", and I'd say, "Nah". I didn't want to go because it was just the clique playing golf and getting pissed and licking Stan's arse. I detached myself from the clique, but you could see how they'd take over and the same players were being picked every week, no matter how well they'd played.

In Stan's second season at the club we got promoted, but we certainly weren't expecting that and I don't think that was the plan. But go up we did and I got 27 goals, so I'd bagged a lot of goals in my two seasons at the club under Stan.

Towards the end of that second season under Stan, it was on my mind that my contract was up in the summer and as I was then 32 years old, it was critical that something was sorted. Ian Wright had arrived, but I was still scoring and it was now only six weeks to the end of the season.

All that had been done was Stan saying to me, "Your contract's up at end of season, isn't it?", and when I said yes, he said, "I'll sort you out". That wasn't really good enough, because, of course, I had a mortgage to pay.

We were by no means certain of promotion, but we had also been signing players such as Steve Davis, who was on

£3,000 a week, which was twice as much as me. I knew quite a few players were on a lot more than I was on and I just felt, if I did really well, I should be rewarded and my pay brought into line with the others.

We played Wrexham away towards the end of the season and I scored my 200th career goal and 50th goal for Burnley, so I thought I'd try to turn the situation to my advantage. Radio Lancashire was interviewing me after the game and the Evening Telegraph and Burnley Express were there, and they asked, "Andy, have you heard anything? Have they offered you anything?", and I said, "No. I haven't been offered anything. Fact."

Anyway, on the coach home, Stan put the Radio Lancashire phone-in on and one fan rang up saying: "What the hell's going on? Why has Andy Payton not been offered a contract?" Then the next caller said: "I can't believe Andy Payton has not been offered a contract. He's the best player this club's got." Stan just sat there and kept the radio on. I was cringing, but it was fair comment. Wright had been dropped to the bench and hadn't scored and I was banging them in and there was still no offer.

We got back to Turf Moor and Stan says, "Can I have a word with you?", and I said, "Course you can."

I thought he was going to explode. He said: "What are you fucking on about saying you haven't been offered a contract? I said I'd sort you out."

"Sort me out? We haven't even talked fucking figures," I replied.

"I said I'd sort you out," he barked.

"We haven't even talked," I said.

"Oh, fuck off," he shouted, and just stormed off.

"You fuck off," I replied.

At training on Monday, he was trying to blank me, but we were doing some finishing and I was on fire. Bang, bang, bang, bang, the shots were going in. At the end of the day I knew I'd got under his skin, but all I was doing was scoring goals and doing a job for the team.

I had a feeling he was just trying to replace me and I was right. I don't know why he got like that, but Stan's like that if you cross him, which I hadn't really meant to do. I was the lad who got 50 goals in two years, so I did as much as him to get us up; but I think Stan just wanted everyone to think it was him who had taken them up.

When I won the Golden Boot Award for the division, obviously I had to go down to the Savoy in London to the big awards ceremony and dinner and I flew down from Manchester with my brother; but not one person from the club went down. You'd have thought they'd have shown some interest.

Anyway, we got to the Savoy and booked into the hotel and on my table were Frank Skinner, Steve Coppell, Garth Crooks and a couple of other celebrities.

There was a woman sat next to me who introduced herself and it turned out she was a journalist from Radio 5 Live. We were talking away for a bit and then she said: "And what do you do for a living?" I said, "I've won the Golden Boot. I'm Andy Payton", and she said: "Oh." She didn't have a clue about Burnley or anything up north and I just thought, "You silly bitch."

Skinner, who, as you know, is a West Brom fan, never spoke. He just chatted to one of his celebrity friends across the table and even when I went up to get my award, he never even asked for a look at it or anything, as you would. I just thought he was a bit of a knobhead. I wasn't that bothered, because it's such a fantastic trophy and when you get one of them you know it's a great achievement.

Jason Roberts, who's now at Blackburn, won the Young Player of the Year award for the division. He was only about 18, but was a right Billy Big Time with all his cronies with him, but I'd won the Golden Boot, so I'd beaten him. I walked back and I said, "All right" to him, but he didn't really want to talk.

My brother and I stayed for a bit, but we ended up going back to the hotel, because I'm not really into all that. But before we went, we spoke to John Motson for a while. He knew Stan and he talked about Burnley coming back from the doldrums and he was sound as a pound. My brother loved it, because he was into football and it made his night.

Most Burnley fans probably recall the signing of Ian Wright as one of the things they most remember about that season. I'd finished training that day and was relaxing at home, knowing I was suspended from the forthcoming Saturday's game because I'd been sent off the previous week.

My next door neighbour, who never even went to Turf Moor, knocked on my door and said: "Have we signed Ian Wright?"

I said: "You what? I've just been at training ground and heard nothing, so we can't have."

I couldn't understand it, but she was right, we had signed

him. I went in next morning and there were 1,000 people watching training and I'm thinking: "Ian Wright? Fucking hell, Ian Wright. Ian Wright's playing in my position on Saturday at home to Wigan. How many goals will he get? Hang on a minute, no disrespect, but I've got 19 goals at this point and all of a sudden if he comes in and does the business, I'm out."

I know that might sound selfish, but I was Burnley's number one striker and I wanted it to stay that way. He was a great guy and all that, but all the lads were arse-licking him beyond belief. You've never seen anything like it. They were star-struck from the moment he came in the first day, giving it all that. Some of them just couldn't believe it; they'd never seen anyone that famous.

Now, don't get me wrong. Ian Wright was a brilliant player, absolutely world class, and I had total respect for him, but he was taking my place, so I didn't want him to succeed. Who would?

If he'd have come in and banged two goals in right away, I might not have got my place back, but I was scoring; so, to put it bluntly, I had the club by the bollocks.

Having said all that, despite all the lads licking his arse, Wrighty was a great bloke and so were his mate and our team-mate Mitchell Thomas, who was sound as a pound.

I'm sure Wright thought Burnley was an absolute shit-hole. He only came up once a week after he had recorded his Friday night TV programme on the Thursday night. It was amazing to think he was interviewing the likes of Caprice and Robert De Niro and then coming to Burnley. He was a multimillionaire and he's had a fantastic career, but he had to do it for Burnley now.

It bugs me a little bit when people say Ian Wright got us up that season, because I got the Golden Boot and 27 league goals, while he got four goals in 15 games. OK, he was great for morale and he might have helped a lot, but the bottom line is: my goals got us promotion. I'm not saying that being big-headed, I am stating a fact.

When we played Gillingham away, I was back up front after scoring in the last two games. Gillingham were joint top with us and they were a good side, and they went one up. Then I equalised and there were the usual muted celebrations as I got about three pats on the back and half the team just ran back. I think it was just that they got that used to me scoring, but at the end of the day you celebrate a goal no matter what.

Anyway, they went 2-1 up and Wrighty has come on as sub and, with 10 minutes to go, the ball bounces round in the box and falls to him. Bang, it's in and, to be fair, he took it really well. But then, for some reason, he set off for Stan, who's stood there waiting for him like he is his long-lost son that he hasn't seen for years. To top it off, the arse-licking brigade are trying to catch him now, hanging off his shirt. I've never seen anything like it. It was unbelievable, considering it was only an equaliser down at Gillingham. There was only me who didn't chase him. I thought: "Oh, bollocks to that."

Stan and Wrighty had been at Palace together for a long time and Stan liked everyone to know he knew him better than anybody and that they loved each other.

We'd had a bit of a falling out do because Stan said he'd sort me out, but we hadn't talked figures; but eventually I went to see him and said I wanted bringing into line with the other players on wages. There were rumours Steve Davis was on £3,000 a week, so I went for double because I knew they were under pressure after I'd won that Golden Boot.

There might have been a few inquiries for me but I was 32, so my age was against me, yet I still thought I was being reasonable with my wage demands. After all, Glen Little told me that he went from £1,500 a week to £7,500 a week a couple of years later. I just wanted rewarding and also to carry on playing for Burnley.

There was talk of interest from Wigan and it was driving me daft, because I just wanted to play for Burnley. I rang Radio Lancashire and got through, so I was speaking live. They were loving it and asked me about the Wigan thing and I was saying I didn't want to play for any other team but Burnley.

Lenny Johnrose was apparently driving home after the game and he said he was nearly spewing when he heard me saying that. I was honest because that's exactly how I felt, but I also did it on purpose because I felt Stan was instigating a few rumours because I knew he was going to want to replace me.

I don't want to turn this into a 'me v Stan' thing, but he signed every man and his dog for a while and I outscored every single one of them, so the fans were just totally behind me.

Eventually, the club had no choice and gave me a new

contract, but there were still problems. There was the story going round that I had a fight with Andy Cooke and Ian Moore, but it wasn't true. I got on with Andy; he was a great lad who appeared on my DVD.

However, I didn't really get on with Ian Moore. He wasn't my cup of tea and I thought he was a soft git who wasn't good enough to replace me. He was quick and he had pace - loads and loads of it - but he couldn't score regularly like I could, and that's a fact. I suppose you wouldn't really expect me to like him because he was taking my place, but I just thought he was loving the fact that he was getting picked instead of me, and he was still being picked, even though he hadn't scored for 10 games.

The club had gone up, so had a massive cash injection and also new sponsorship, so things were moving at Turf Moor; but Steve Davis stubbed my foot accidentally in a pre-season game and I broke my little toe. So I missed the first game of the season away to Bolton when we drew 1-1, with the goal coming from another recent signing in Phil Gray.

Next we played Hartlepool at home in a cup game. I was sub and we were losing 1-0 at half-time, but I came on and scored a hat-trick, and I just kept scoring, eventually getting 15 goals in 18 games. If I'd have played the whole season, I'd have probably got at least 20, if not 30 goals, and it was a crazy situation, with the fans screaming "Get Payton on" every game when I was on the bench, which was more often than not.

I don't know what was going on in Stan's head, but it was like he didn't want to play me for some reason. I once saw him reading a match programme and the week before I'd got a hat-trick, so there were about six pictures of me. I saw Stan pick up and read it, then watched him as he screwed it up and threw it away.

He signed a string of strikers such as Gray, Dimi Papadopoulos, Gareth Taylor, Moore, Tony Ellis and David Johnson. The latter was a good player who was flying at the time, but he was just on too much money.

Taylor would have been good to play with, obviously, because I'd always played off a big man and he was good in the air; but I only got the chance to play with him once, when he did his trademark flick-on and I scored a couple.

One occasion that really sticks in my mind was at training one Friday when we didn't know what the team was going to be, as we'd been on a bad run. The back four set-up and the midfield was decided, but there were five strikers, including myself, Papadopoulos, Moore and Taylor, and Stan was trying all these different combinations in a practice game.

After about an hour, Sam said: "Right, lads. That's it. We are going to have a game now."

So I said: "Er, Sam. Have you forgotten someone? You've just tried every fucking combination of strikers apart from me. I'm stood here warming up, just like everyone else."

He apologised, but it was part of a wider problem, because what was really happening was that he was picking everyone but me time and again. It was a ridiculous situation which should never have happened.

Those last two years at Burnley were an awful time for me. It's a nightmare when you're not playing because you don't feel part of it. It was even worse because I was banging in the goals for the reserves and people were saying: "Oh, Payton's scored again. Why is he not in the team?" It should never have happened and it was a terrible time. To make things worse, I was done for drink-driving at the time, but I almost felt like it was no wonder because the situation was really getting to me.

The summer after we were promoted, we were in the Isle of Man on a pre-season tour and I was talking to chief scout Cliff Roberts.

"Where's Stan?" I said.

"Oh, signing somebody," said Cliff.

"Who? Who is he signing?"

"You won't want to know. He's a striker."

I was thinking: "Why does he need a striker? I've just won the Golden Boot and we don't need a striker because he's got me."

Then Cliff told me it was a Greek Under-21 international who was a good player and was signing for half a million quid tomorrow. I just thought: "Here we go again."

The next day, we were all there at training and Stan's assistant, Sam Ellis, said the new signing was coming, and Dimi appeared. He had shades on, a denim jacket with the collar up and tight jeans on, and he just looked a complete dick. It was so funny and most of the lads were pissing themselves.

But Dimi was a great lad and a good player as well. Unfortunately, he just did too much diving and the fact that he couldn't speak any English at all was a big problem for him. To be honest, I don't know why Stan bought him, because he ended up hardly playing him.

We had a mixed season, but got to the quarter-finals of the FA Cup and were drawn away to Watford. They were a similar side to us, so we had a great chance to get to the FA Cup semi-finals.

Steve Davis had been out for three months and hadn't even played a reserve game, but Stan in his wisdom named him among the subs, while I was overlooked and so was Dimi, even though he'd scored two in a practice match on the Thursday and looked really sharp.

As myself and Dimi were not involved, we went into the players' lounge and watched the game on TV and we could see it was all going wrong. We went a goal down and we needed a goal, but we had no strikers. It was soul-destroying for us, and even worse when Stan brought Davis on and put him up front. He could hardly run and it was ridiculous, and I felt Stan was just hoping he'd score so people would say it was an inspired substitution.

Dimi was saying: "Andy, why, why?"

"Dimi, I haven't got a clue, mate," I replied. "It's scandalous. You are definitely on form and should have been playing."

It was such a massive let down for the club because it was a diabolical performance. You need strikers to win a game and we just didn't perform, which was so frustrating for me. Stan stuck to his favourites and seemed to keep the players who played golf with him and it was horrible at times.

We signed Paul Gascoigne later that year, which was

another unbelievable signing for the club. At the time, Gazza was at Everton, although he hadn't been in their side, and loads of pressmen turned up at the Gawthorpe training ground because it was such a massive signing.

Gazza came in for the training session with his big mate Jimmy 'Five Bellies', who drove him round and looked after him. He didn't really speak much, but obviously at the time he was struggling in his personal life with alcohol problems. I don't want to knock him in any way because he was one of my favourite players, but at that particular time in his life he was struggling to combine both playing and dealing with his drinking.

In one of the first training sessions which was being taken by one of our coaches, Mick Docherty, we were doing something quite simple, running from the corner flag to the ball in the centre, but Gazza was really struggling. I was watching him and I think, looking back now, in my personal opinion, he was under the influence. The players could tell straight away it wasn't the Gazza of old and we knew it was going to be a bad signing because he wasn't going to have any real influence on the team.

One of the first away games in which Gazza was involved was down at Portsmouth and we all turned up on the Friday for the long journey down in track suits. Gazza had a brown doctor's bag, where we all had claret and blue kit bags.

He sat right in front of me all the way down and eventually curiosity got the better of me and I said to him: "What have you brought that bag for?"

"I'll show you on the way back," was his reply and those were his exact words.

Anyway, we got down there very late as usual and went straight to bed. When we got up in the morning, the team was announced and as usual I wasn't even sub, so it was a case of me watching the game from the stands, while Gazza was on the bench.

We drew the game and I think the manager was quite pleased with the result; so we've stopped at the off-licence on the way back to get a few beers for the long journey home, which we sometimes did if we got a good result.

Gazza bought 18 WKDs, filling his doctor's bag, and by the time we got past Birmingham, he was absolutely paralytic. He came to life and he was doing card tricks and all the lads were egging him on, and, to be fair, he was funny. There was all sorts of silliness going on and at one point I rang my mates and put Gazza on the phone. Stan, however, stayed out of it and just sat at the front of the bus all the way back.

Gazza was sub every game, but did very little for us. Hindsight is a wonderful thing, but looking back, we should have put a story that he'd damaged his knee and couldn't play or something like that. We only missed the play-offs by one goal and we might have done it with a different line-up, because Gazza did nothing for us really. He almost scored with a free kick when he came on as sub in the final game against Coventry, but it was too little too late.

My prediction that even when I signed that new contract I would be eased out of the equation was coming true, even though I was scoring goals. I got 15 that season in 18 games and when you think Jay Rodriguez was top scorer for Burnley last season with the same number in a full season, it shows I was still performing.

But Stan just would not play me. It was crazy and I still don't know why it happened. At the time, he said he wanted younger players in and he wanted a new direction, but I was still scoring goals and that was the thing that killed it for me.

It was starting to get really demoralising and, though I told him I didn't want to go out on loan, looking back that might have been a good thing, because at least then I'd have been playing football. When you are training all week and doing your best and you are just not getting picked, it really is a nightmare, especially when people come up to you all the time and ask why you are not involved, and you can't give them an answer.

The second to last game of the season was away to Sheffield United and there was always going to be a bit of needle because Stan and Blades' boss Neil Warnock didn't like each other. It nearly kicked off in the dressing room at half-time; there were things going on between Stan and Warnock, and Stan was trying to get Ronnie Jepson down out of the stands with Lenny Johnrose as a sort of back-up. I came on as sub but didn't do much and we lost 2-0, which almost put us out of the play-off picture.

It had got to the point where I wasn't being selected, but I knew there were players being chosen week in week out that weren't playing particularly well, and it got really demoralising. It was a 'catch-22' situation because I didn't want to leave the club as I'd made it clear I was Burnley through and through and wanted to finish my career with the club. I wanted to get to 100 goals for the club, but that was never going to happen because I wasn't being picked.

It sounds like I was being paranoid, but it got to the stage where I wasn't even being selected for the reserves because if I scored it would then put the management under pressure to explain why I wasn't being picked. We were still signing strikers because Robbie Blake had arrived, but they couldn't get rid of me and they knew I could still score goals.

The fact that Kevin Phillips is still playing and still scoring goals proves my point. I was younger than he is now as I was only 34, but I wasn't being given the opportunity and it was demoralising.

Eventually, I did go out to Blackpool on loan for a spell, but it didn't really help matters. I was earning £3,000 a week, which wasn't mega-money but wasn't bad, but I was really down because a footballer needs to play in front of the crowd to keep the weekly buzz going. I felt as though the staff knew what they were doing and just wouldn't play me, and I found it really difficult to accept.

I was told I had to go to Blackpool on loan the day after I had been arrested for drink-driving, which brought both myself and the club bad publicity. I accept it was wrong and would never defend what I did; but, looking back now, it wasn't the end of the world. Fellow ex-Burnley player Clarke Carlisle has just been convicted of the same offence and he's put it behind him.

Stan informed me that the chairman wanted me out of the club, which I found a bit hard to believe, considering my scoring record; but Blackpool boss Steve McMahon came in for me and it was already a done deal by the time I heard about it. Steve had tried to sign me before when he was Swindon manager.

It was obviously an embarrassing time, because everyone knew I had been done for drink-driving, so I felt like putting a bag over my head. But Blackpool were doing OK at the time and the ground was being redeveloped, and I settled into a routine with my brother driving me over, as clearly I wasn't allowed to drive myself.

I'd scored a lot of goals against Blackpool, so quite a lot of their fans didn't like me anyway, but I settled in and did all right, scoring in an away game at Bury. I found it really hard, to be honest, as I wasn't match fit because I'd not been playing, end of story. After that game at Bury, which ended 1-1, I said in a radio interview that I wanted to come back to Burnley because I was missing the place.

Yet when I did come back, I feel almost as though I was an embarrassment to the club. People could see I was still useful because I'd scored a goal while on loan, but I think most of the staff at Burnley were gutted that I had come back and the situation went straight back to how it was before me not being involved in anything, and it stayed like that until my contract was up.

Stan had stopped playing me and I think I became a little bit of a boil on his arse, because when I was scoring people were asking him why he wasn't playing me. It became a really raw 'them and us' situation. Stan stuck to his guns and said he wanted younger players in, and it was just a horrible scenario for both myself and the club.

Rumours started flying round about clashes between me and Stan and about things I'd done, but none of them were true. All I did was turn up for training and keep hoping to play so I could get up to my 100 goals for the club. As I said, they made sure that was never going to happen because I wasn't playing, and I eventually finished up with 82 goals for Burnley, just 18 short of my target.

Looking back, I was only 34 at the time and still very fit, so I think I would easily have done it if I had played regularly those last two seasons. But it's history now and so there's no point dwelling on it.

In the very last game of the season before my contract ran out, Stan asked me if I wanted to make an appearance, but I turned it down. I felt I'd done so much for the club and then had hardly been picked for two years, so I felt a bit insulted that he'd asked me, because it seemed just a novelty offer. I didn't want the fans thinking everything was OK.

I went on the pitch at the end and waved to the fans, who chanted my name, which was great and very emotional, but it was with mixed feelings, as I hadn't played for two years. I still believe the club created that situation and it was hard to take, so it was hardly a fine farewell, even though I still loved the club.

My Summary

We had a guy called Ally Pickering on loan from Stoke City who had played about 400 games for the Potters and had been a real stalwart full-back there. We played Stoke at their place that season and Ally got a good reception from the home fans because he had given them some loyal service. His dad had died a day or two before the game and he wasn't going to play, but said he wanted to go out there in memory of his father.

It was unbelievable how it turned out, because Ally never usually scored, but he hit a volley from about 40 yards right into the top corner. It was an amazing strike and was fitting that it happened at Stoke. He was so emotional because it was for his dad and everyone responded to it and it was a magical moment.

We went through a period around that time where we were getting a lot of triallists in. Most of them had not been good enough and you could more or less tell straight away.

But then we got a French lad on trial who couldn't speak much English and you could tell straight away in his first training session he looked the part. We found out his name was Arthur Gnohere, and he was strong, had pace and wanted to get on with the lads. He ended up being signed and broke into the first team and did really well. He was a bit of a man-mountain and the fans loved him.

When he got in the team he was really flying and one of the best signings Stan made, especially as we got him on a free. He scored a brilliant goal in a televised game at Preston, which involved a couple of one-twos, and was playing superbly.

The thing with Arthur was that I think it all must have gone to his head a little bit. He apparently had some off-the-field problems, including getting divorced, but it just all got a bit weird. He bought two cars, an X5 and another brand-new BMW, but I don't know why, because why would you need two cars? His career just sort of came to a standstill as quickly as it had taken off and he left soon afterwards.

Looking at my career in general for a second, and one of the quirkiest and most remarkable facts was that I scored both the first and last Football League goals of the Nineties.

The first was on New Year's Day, 1990, when Hull City was at home to Sunderland. I'd just broken into the first team and was playing really well. The police had told the club to bring the kick-off forward to 11am because they were expecting such a big crowd and a huge away following.

It was the first game of the day and the first game of the new decade, and I scored the first goal, putting the ball past Sunderland's ex-Burnley keeper Tony Norman, in a cracking game we went on to win 3-2.

Fast forward 10 years to the end of December, 1999, and I was in the Burnley team which played Oxford at home. I got a hat-trick and scored the winning goal in the 93rd minute, therefore scoring the last and first goals of the decade, which is unbelievable. The Jimmy McIlroy Stand was officially opened that afternoon and it was a great day, with Jimmy Mac and loads of great ex-players on the pitch before the game.

As far as career achievements go, winning the Golden Boot Award for being top scorer in the whole Football League and helping Burnley get promoted has got to be number one. I later donated my golden boot to charity and Burnley FC won it in the auction, which is kind of another story later on. I don't think you will get many ex-professionals giving their golden boot trophy away. I was also proud of the fact that I got 25 league goals for Hull City when they finished bottom of the league. Only one of those 25 was a penalty and I think, if I had been regular penalty taker, I could have won the Golden Boot that year as well! I was only three behind Teddy Sheringham, who I believe won it that year. To do that playing for a club which finished bottom would have been remarkable.

Signing for Celtic was also a memorable moment, especially as I went on to be top scorer that season and scored the winner in an Old Firm game, which really put me on the map. I've always said one regret was that I didn't stay longer at Celtic, but maybe I wouldn't have got the chance to play for Burnley if I had.

Leaving home at 16 and living in digs and still making it is also something I am very proud of, because you are just a kid at that age and it's really hard. My daughter Olivia is 14 now and I was only two years older than her when I left home, so it really makes me think how tough it was.

Coming to Burnley was obviously also a great memory, especially as they were rock bottom at the time and it was a big gamble to sign for them; but doing the business for them was brilliant, though to be honest I enjoyed the whole of my career.

The best ground I played at was Old Trafford, when I turned out for Celtic in Pat Bonner's testimonial. It was a fantastic experience because Celtic took 40,000 fans down to the game. The game was a draw, as testimonials often are, but the likes of Gordon Strachan and Roy Keane were in the United team and, though I wasn't on the field that long, it was just an amazing experience playing in front of that massive full house.

The worst ground I've played at would have to be Bristol Rovers' Memorial Ground. I remember that being a diabolical pitch because it was also Bristol's rugby union ground. When I played for Hull, we drew 0-0 there and it was the first game of the season. It was an absolutely boiling hot day and the ground was rock hard and just horrible to play on.

The managers who have had most influence on me? Brian Horton is obviously one, because the first five years of my career were all about him. He taught me well and gave me the opportunity in football, so I have got to be thankful to him for that; plus I have to say he was a really good manager.

Liam Brady too was great. Obviously, he's a world-famous player who had a host of Italian championship medals, so for him to sign you is a compliment in itself. He had tried to get me twice before and got me the third time, so it's a great feeling that someone like that wants you to play for him.

I also have to mention Stan Ternent, because at the end of the day I was flying in my first two years at Burnley and it was only when myself and Stan started having problems and he stopped playing me that things went wrong.

Chris Waddle too is worth mentioning, because he brought me back to Burnley, and if it hadn't been for him I would never have got the chance to play for the club I love; and Danny Wilson at Barnsley was good. But, all in all, I'd have to say Stan was the best manager I played under.

Probably one of the worst managers in my opinion was Terry Dolan at Hull, though that's mainly because I personally learned very little from him. He didn't last long in that job anyway and to me he had no personality and seemed more suited to working in an office than being a manager.

As for favourite goals, my first in league football in the second minute of Hull's home game against Leeds is clearly one, as is the goal I scored two minutes into my debut for Middlesbrough, when I was put clean through, so was under a lot of pressure: one against one with the keeper, but took it round him and put it in.

My first Celtic goal in my second game for them, which secured a 1-0 win, was also memorable, as of course was the Old Firm winner, and so was my first goal for Burnley, which came in my home debut against Southend. It really took the pressure off me. My last goal of the promotion season at home to Cambridge was also fantastic, as it clinched me the Golden Boot.

My worst moment in football, even though I knew it was coming, was the day my career finished, i.e. when my contract was up at Burnley. Everyone had got used to me not playing and I was just turning up to watch, so it was horrible near the end and really soul destroying. If you're a professional footballer, packing in playing feels like part of you has died. You feel as though part of you is no longer there and it is really demoralising.

As far as players I respected, Kevin Keegan and Gary Lineker were the ones I really looked up to because they were the best players around at that time. Lineker was top scorer in the 1986 World Cup and Keegan was European Player of the Year twice in a row.

When I was at Hull City, we had a player called Keith Edwards, who had scored 250 goals, so I looked up to him. I always asked him a lot of questions and learned from him, because he was just an out-and-out goalscorer.

You always respect fellow strikers, especially top-class ones, but generally you concentrate on your own game and trying to bring out the best in yourself.

My favourite football strip was certainly not Hull's. They play in black and amber and we had some really bad strips when I was there. But I really liked the Celtic strip because it is so unique. To put on the green and white hoops was fantastic, because they really drummed into you how much it meant to put on that famous shirt.

I've also got to include every Burnley top I wore and played in, as it was my home town team; to wear the famous claret and blue top meant the world to me.

My match-day routine always started with getting up early and having a light breakfast. A lot of players just stuffed their faces, but I liked to play on an empty stomach, as I didn't want to be running round with a load of sausages and beans inside me. I'd have a bit of cereal and that would be it. It's all about sharpness and I always felt sharper, obviously, when I had an empty stomach. Sometimes, if you were away from home and you knew you'd only be a sub, you'd go down to breakfast in the hotel and it would all be laid out. It was really tempting to stuff your face, but you would be warming up half an hour later and preparing to go on, so you were in trouble. I've seen players caught out like that, so never fell into the trap.

My best ever XI

Goalkeeper

It would have to be either Celtic's Pat Bonner or ex-Burnley keeper Marlon Beresford. 'Packie' was a good keeper and earned around 100 Irish caps, but Marlon impressed me and was an excellent penalty stopper who saved around half the spot-kicks he faced. So I think I'd go for Marlon.

Right back

Tom Boyd. He bagged around 100 Scottish caps and was such a great athlete, he could run all day long. He was so good on the overlap he could do it with a cigar in his mouth. He had a great temperament and, like all the Celtic players, was 100 per cent dedicated. It rubbed off on you when you saw one player doing a bit extra and you knew everyone did; that is what you find at the big clubs.

Centre backs

I only saw him late in his career, but Gary Gillespie was in the Alan Hansen mould, and what a compliment that is. He was very wiry and about 6ft 3ins tall, but had pace and could pass the ball brilliantly and read a game superbly. He was part of that all-conquering Liverpool team and, though I didn't play against him, I admired his silky skills.

My other centre half would be Tony Mowbray, who was a lot rawer than Gillespie, but always wore his heart on his sleeve and was true captain material. He would steam into challenges and put his head through a brick wall for the team if he had to. He was just a great guy who overcame a lot of personal tragedy in his life.

Left back

I've gone for Dariusz Wdowczyk, who was a Polish International with about 50 caps. He was at Celtic when I was there. His legs were like tree trunks, but he could whip a ball in and not many people would get any change out of him defensively.

Midfield

First choice and my captain is Paul McStay. He stayed at Celtic, even though Liverpool and a host of other clubs wanted him and he could have gone anywhere. He was an absolutely great player and a gentleman as well. As a churchgoer, he wouldn't swear, but he would have the crack and was a hell of a player.

Alongside him, I'd have another Celtic man in John Collins. He was such a fitness fanatic, he literally had a 12-pack! He was another totally dedicated player who went on to play for Monaco, and it was good to see people like that at the club, because it makes you want to emulate them.

My final midfield choice is Neil Redfearn, who was at Barnsley with me. Neil scored loads of goals from midfield, many of them spectacular long shots, and he always wanted to be top scorer instead of me, so we had some great banter. He was a great lad and a very good player.

Strikers

Up front, I'd have Charlie Nicholas, who scored when Arsenal beat Liverpool in that memorable 1987 League Cup Final. He was unbelievably skilful and had great tight control, even better than Robbie Blake, who is also a great player and came close to my starting 11; but Charlie just beats him to it. Charlie was a fantastic player and a nice guy as well. I've also gone for Frank McAvennie, who was a great striker to play off and would guarantee you a good night out afterwards. Frank was a well-respected striker. Finally, I'd obviously put myself in between them to complete the XI.

My Least favourite starting XI

Goalkeeper

I've gone for Frank Kvaal, who came to Burnley on a trial basis under Stan Ternent, who had only just taken over and took a chance on him and didn't know how bad he was, unfortunately.

We were playing an FA Cup tie against Darlington, which was being played at Middlesbrough as Darlington had ground problems. They were really struggling and Stan expected us to win comfortably. It looked like he was right, because we were 2-0 up and I had scored both goals; but then I got sent off. It was a dodgy decision, because I got a yellow card for abusing a linesman when I was miles away and hardly said anything, then got a second yellow for sliding in on the keeper, who did the old flip and fooled the ref, when I didn't touch him.

However, there were only 10 minutes to go, so I thought we'd surely hang on, and went to the dressing room. I heard a bit of a roar and knew it was 2-1, but there were only four minutes left then, so I thought we were still OK. Then I heard another roar in the 90th minute and I thought: "Bastards. A draw." There were two minutes of injury time and then I thought, "Surely not!", because Frank tried to save one with his legs when he should have used his hands and it was 3-2 and we were out of the cup.

Stan's reaction was one of disbelief, but the lad couldn't speak English and just put his hands up as a gesture of apology and probably didn't realise what a big deal it was to go out of the FA Cup. He got found out big style and left the club soon after, never to be seen again. He was a nice lad, but he wasn't up to it.

Right back

Chris Brass won 'own goal of the season' three years on the bounce and the one where he hits the ball into his own face and it goes in for an own goal is hilarious. I really liked Chris, so it's a reluctant choice, but anyone with any quality would destroy him.

Centre backs

I've gone for Steve Blatherwick, who was at Nottingham Forest at one time, so must have been doing OK; but on the evidence of what I saw at Burnley, he was pretty shocking. He was a huge bloke and could get nasty, but his performances for us were terrible.

Alongside him, I've chosen Gordon Armstrong. He had played for Sunderland in an FA Cup Final and had a decent career, but I never really got on with him because he always thought he could talk down to everyone and thought he was a bit special. Stan played him as a sort of sweeper, but I would have loved to play against him all day long because he couldn't run and always favoured the left side, because he was very left-footed. Because he'd been captain at Bury, I think he just automatically thought he'd been given a bit of licence to be captain and an authority, but I just didn't get on with him and I didn't rate him either.

Left back

A lad called Steve Morgan played for Burnley when I was there. He was stocky and aggressive and a bit of an animal, but his distribution was atrocious and his football ability was shocking.

Midfield

I've gone for Mark Ford, who was an ex-England under-21 captain; but when he came to Burnley he just looked like a little lad who was going to get the piss taken out of him. He gave me the impression he didn't want to be at the club and he never performed for us.

Also in midfield, I'd put Mark Winstanley, who didn't give a toss about Burnley. I can remember once when I arrived at the training ground and he parked at the side of me and, to strike up a conversation, I asked if he watched the game yesterday on TV and he replied with, "I don't like football".

Very strange bloke, in my opinion. He just wanted summer to come so he could go and do whatever he wanted. In one game, he crossed the ball behind the net four times. The fans were going spare and they'd every right to, because you expect better quality than that if you've paid good money to get into the game.

Finally, I'd have Michael Williams, a lad we got from Sheffield Wednesday. He looked quite tricky, but he had a bad time at Burnley and everything went downhill from there. His confidence went completely and I think Stan got on his case a little bit. He was a Waddle signing and he probably thought, because he was doing OK at Wednesday, he could play at our level; but once he was out of his comfort zone, his confidence went completely.

Strikers

I've put Ian Moore in because I just didn't like him. To be fair, I didn't mind him as a lad, but it was just the fact that he took my place and he knew it and also knew that I could do nothing about it. I thought he was a bit smarmy and a bit of a mard-arse. When Stan signed him for more than a million pounds from Stockport, we were expecting something special; but he clearly wasn't. I think Stan, with hindsight, wouldn't have signed him, especially as he had told everyone the week before that he definitely wasn't signing him.

Alongside Moore, I'd put Lee Howey, who had also played in other positions for us. Howey occasionally played up front and, in my opinion, he was poor in most of the positions he was told to play in.

I'm going to put Graham Branch in for the last place, even

though he played anywhere under Stan. He was centre-half, left back, up front. You name it, he played there, and he was a great lad. But he was another one with a confidence crisis always lurking in his head and he was always looking for an excuse as to why he hadn't played that well and analysing his performances too much.

When I finished playing, I had a stint on the Football in the Community programme and around that time I was asked to play for Colne FC.

The community work was tough because, come 9 o'clock in the morning, there would be 40 kids at the gym behind the James Hargreaves Stand at Burnley and the parents would leave them and come back five hours later. They were all different abilities and some just couldn't kick a ball, and it was like babysitting really and very frustrating. It was hard work to put anything constructive on, because half the time you were breaking up fights. The lads got trophies just for being there, which was part of the idea of the scheme, but it didn't really appeal to me and I only stuck it out for about a month.

But it was during that work that it came home to me that I wasn't a professional player any more. You'd be standing in the middle of the pitch and it would just come into your head that you're not playing any more and you haven't got a game to look forward to on Saturday.

Kids talked to me in the past tense about when I played, and even though I'd only just finished playing, you would get kids saying, "What's your name and who did you play for?", even though we were right next to Burnley's ground; while a few months before everyone knew me and I was always being asked for my autograph. I felt like I'd become a has-been and 'yesterday's hero', and I found it very depressing.

At that time, I also had a spell doing this 'speed ball' challenge. It was a fundraiser run by Chairman Barry Kilby and the school got half the money raised. It basically involved the kids kicking a ball as hard as they could and seeing who could get the fastest speed. It was in a good cause, but there was no skill involved and the equipment looked faulty to me some of the time because some kids would get a good score after hardly kicking the ball. All in all, it was a bit boring.

The move to play for Colne came about through a lad we called Webby, who had been an apprentice at Burnley but was released and went on to become a local golf professional. His dad was Chairman of Colne and offered me £200 a week, which for that club I presume would have been a lot of money.

I hesitated, but decided to go up to see what training was like; but when I got there and saw the facilities and the sloping pitch, I really didn't fancy it after the great grounds I'd played on for so many years. Their manager was Nigel Coates, who had been in the post for years and wasn't very inspiring and was very deadpan.

I reluctantly decided to give it a go, but it was eerie going into the dressing room. All the lads knew who I was and my record, but nobody really let on. I played one game away to Nelson on a Tuesday night and a few people had come down to watch. I was put clean through and scored and there was a bit of a ripple of applause, but I recall it being just like slow motion. As I turned away after scoring, I saw a bloke walking his dog along a path by the ground, and I compared it to scoring for Burnley and the whole crowd going up, and made up my mind there and then not to play for them again.

I wasn't in the right frame of mind and it wasn't football as I had been used to. I wasn't really fit either, as I hadn't been training, so I told the manager: "Look, at the end of the day I'll be absolutely straight with you. I'm not going to take any money off you, but I just can't get up for it. I didn't get a buzz out there scoring against Nelson, so I'll just leave it."

It was just a nothing game for me and didn't even compare with playing in a reserve game for a professional club. I meant no disrespect and it probably meant a great deal to play for Colne for the lads who were turning out for them, but it meant nothing to me because it was the end of my career.

Having said that, the last few months at Burnley were awful for me. Throughout my career, I'd always be first in and get there too early sometimes, just because I was so excited and getting ready to play. But week after week I was going into the dressing room, waiting for Stan to put the team on the board and then the subs, and my name wasn't there. I'd say: "All the best, lads", but inside I was all over the place and it was just soul-destroying.

I definitely think something went wrong in my head at that time, though I don't know if it went as far as a nervous breakdown; but I missed playing football so much and became really depressed.

Then Brian Miller's son David, who was manager of Stalybridge Celtic at the time, rang me up and asked me if I wanted to sign for them, so out of courtesy I went over with him to have a look around. To be fair, it wasn't a bad little set-up, but, once again, the timing was wrong and I wasn't right mentally. I didn't want to play for Stalybridge, even though there were a few lads who I knew there, and we never got as far as discussing wages.

I was gambling heavily by this time and I still had loads of money from my playing days, so I had the cash to waste. But I was losing most of it and I might as well have just gone into the bookies and given them a few hundred quid over the counter and said: "Right, I'll see you tomorrow." You can get a bit of a buzz from gambling and there can be a bit of a social aspect too, in that you might meet one of the lads in the bookies and can get chatting about one thing and another. But let's face it, you are literally giving them your money and there is only one winner in the end, and that's the bookie.

A lot of footballers have fallen foul of gambling and I was one of them. My daily routine became getting up and going to the bookies to put some more bets on; but I just carried on.

I was also putting on weight because I wasn't training. I'd started to get unfit when I was still at Burnley because of how Stan treated me. He was really cute the way he did it, in that he said he wasn't playing me in the reserves and then had an excuse not to pick me because he said I wasn't match fit. I ended up standing around at training watching the first team doing what they call pattern play, which was mostly just running exercises.

This went on for months and Stan tried to move me on by giving me an option to go on loan, but I made sure that didn't happen because, just to be stubborn and get my own back, I thought, "I'm going nowhere. I'm going to show everyone round here they can't treat me like that." So it just became a stalemate.

I don't think it was that which caused my depression. I think just finishing playing hits most footballers that way because when you are playing you feel great, but when you stop there's just nothing to replace it.

I went through a real bad patch and learned things the hard way, but I know it was still all my own fault. I was in the bookies all the time and was also lending people large amounts of money, and some of those I lent cash to I hardly knew. People got to thinking: "Oh, he's minted, we can ask him for owt." I'm a generous person and always have been, but you find out when you're in such a situation that, firstly, you don't get your money back, and secondly, if you do go after people for the cash, you've no chance.

I was also being asked for tickets all the time, and I felt like Del Boy at times because folk were asking for football boots and things like that, and I think people thought I had a room full of signed tops. I could get a few tickets sometimes, but that was it, and I was really being used.

I was also being asked all the time to do presentations at junior football clubs and other functions, and all I'd get as far as payment went was a couple of free drinks. I remember doing one at Turf Moor for a junior team from Worsthorne, and there were about 300 kids there and I was on the stage for three hours, shaking hands and presenting trophies. I obviously wasn't expecting any payment, but it was three hours hard work just for a cheer at the end.

I got to thinking people were taking the piss out of me really. I couldn't refuse any requests, otherwise everyone would say I was an arrogant tosser or similar things.

What I'll say now is that money is easily spent and I found myself thinking it was never going to dry up. When you have always earned and earned well, as I did for 20 years, you still keep spending like you are still earning big, even when the money has dried up. You don't want people to think that you are slowing down a bit because you are no longer a footballer and living in the dream. You want people to think you are still minted and you still keep spending. There would be times when I might be in the bookies with £200 on me and I was flashing it about just to let people know I still had money and that I wasn't on skid row, because people are always asking questions.

But, eventually, you begin to realise the money is getting spent and you know it's running out, yet you just carry on so you don't lose face. If I could go back in time, I'd have looked after it a lot better, but what's done is done.

I ended up signing on because I was looking to do some work to earn the money that I wasted. I wasn't really doing anything, apart from looking after my daughters, and eventually I was offered a job through an agency as a bin man. Word must have got round because at 6 o'clock the following morning I walked into the canteen at the depot I was sent to and it all went quiet. But there were no fly comments or anything. The people there just wanted to see how I handled myself, and I was OK, because I was as sound as a pound workwise.

It wasn't great money, around £170 take home, but that's how hard it got. I was grateful for the work, because at the end of the day I was skint. Despite what people might think, I didn't earn millions of pounds in my career and I certainly realised that at this point.

One of my jobs was emptying the bins of dog shit and a couple of years ago, when it was really cold, about minus 18, all the bins were frozen and you had to bang them on the top to get them open and everything inside was rock hard, so it was really hard work at times and not very pleasant. It was obviously very humbling and I was thinking: "Do I wear a baseball cap and a scarf so I won't get seen?" because I didn't want any comments or anything else. Eventually, I thought "Bollocks to it" and just got on with it. As it happened, nobody said anything offensive anyway, though a few did say things like, "Oh my God. Why are you doing that sort of thing?", and I'd reply: "I'm doing it cos I love it."

They were a good set of lads at the depot and I clearly was in no position to give it the Billy Big Time, so I got on OK with them all; but it made me realise I should have looked after my money a lot better.

I was still having problems and wasn't in the right frame of mind to get myself together and, looking back, I realise I should have sought help and try to find someone to point me in the right direction.

I didn't go to matches at Turf Moor as I found it so hard

because I wasn't playing any more, but there were spells when the team was doing well and I found myself thinking I didn't want the players there now to do as well as me, even though, of course, I wanted Burnley to do well. It was a really confusing feeling.

You are forgotten so quickly. One minute you are the hero and man of the match, and all that, and the next minute the same people don't look at you because you're not a player any more. If people watch my DVD, they might think, "Bloody hell, Payton was a decent player", but kids in Burnley nowadays are probably saying Jay Rodriguez is miles better than me because you are easily forgotten when you pack in playing.

The PFA are talking about introducing schemes to help players when they quit, and that's a great move and is long overdue.

The statistics are frightening for ex-players. Many hit the bottle and there have even been some suicides, and one survey showed something like 85 per cent of marriages involving footballers between the ages of 35 and 40 break down.

That sort of thing happens because you are just like a fish out of water when you finish playing. If I had bought something to go into, such as a fitness centre or gym or something similar, I may have been OK, but I didn't and just ended up doing nothing all day. I had money at first and could have done plenty of things, but I was just waking up every day, going out to get the Racing Post and going to the bookies, and it was just a horrible downward spiral. That's what football does to you. It's so big and it's your life, but when it spits you out, that's it.

I could walk down to Burnley's training ground at Gawthorpe or go to Turf Moor and if I went in the dressing rooms, nobody would know who I was, which is so hard to handle after being a hero a few years before. Little things you take for granted also bring the situation home, such as on a match day when you'd get tickets and a parking spot with no problems; but then, when you leave the club, all that suddenly stops.

I started playing locally for pub teams and enjoying playing football again and working with kids, getting them to improve their shooting and other aspects of the striker's trade. I found out that I still loved the game and it really does give me a big buzz and makes me feel I've turned the corner at last.

A couple of my daughters play football now and I had to pull myself together for them and be a good dad for them. The girls are growing up fast and it's amazing that Olivia is 14 now and in two years she will be leaving school.

I also hope to start driving again. I'm free to get my licence back and it's just a matter of applying.

I feel OK now and I'm in a hell of a lot better place than when I stopped playing, even though I had a lot more money then. I was just not right then and I got a bit bitter and twisted because I wasn't playing any more. I started thinking the club could have treated me better, but when you are the local lad, you're always the centre of attention and that can go against you a little bit sometimes because everyone thinks they know you and they take advantage of you.

But my priority at the moment is very much looking after my daughters and that's my main responsibility. They all live with me at the moment and they are great girls and, as I said, growing up very fast.

I've now started managing Burnley Grammar School Old Boys FC, but I'd like to manage at a higher grade, just locally, even if it's at Ramsbottom, Padiham or another non-league side at that kind of level. At least people know I'm keeping my eye in now and not just doing nothing, and if we do well, you never know who might notice.

I was asked to take on the GSOB job and it was nice to feel wanted again. I've taken a few training sessions and improved their training straight away because they weren't really doing anything; they are struggling, so I want to get them back on the winning track, because that's what you get judged on, and hopefully it will be a stepping stone to better things. I'll just see what happens and try and enjoy it.

I'm enjoying my football again now and will enjoy it even more if we start winning, because I don't want to be associated with a team at the bottom of the league, which is where we are now.

Olivia is playing football and doing well and Georgia plays for the school, and, all in all, things are definitely looking up.

I've made mistakes, but every mistake I've made has been well documented and I don't ever want to see any bad headlines again. After all, I have got my kids to think about and they would get slaughtered, wouldn't they?

So yes, I'm back on track, and I'm still Burnley to the core and Burnley's very own Natural Born Claret (that's another story). My first edition book details my past, good and bad. I've lived my dream, so here's to the future ...

Season	Club	League			F A Cup			League Cup			Europe			Other			Total		
		Full	Sub	Goals	Full	Sub	Goals	Full	Sub	Goals	Full	Sub	Goals	Full	Sub	Goals	Full	Sub	Goals
1986-87	Hull City	-	2	-	-	-	-	-	-	-	-	-	-	-	-	-	-	2	-
1987-88	Hull City	11	11	2	3	-	-	-	1	-	-	-	-	-	-	-	14	12	2
1988-89	Hull City	18	10	4	3	-	-	1	1	-	-	-	-	-	-	-	22	11	4
1989-90	Hull City	34	5	17	1	-	-	2	-	1	-	-	-	1	-	-	38	5	18
1990-91	Hull City	43	-	25	1	-	-	3	-	-	-	-	-	1	-	-	48	-	25
1991-92	Hull City	10	-	7	-	-	-	3	-	1	-	-	-	1	-	-	14	-	8
Total		**116**	**28**	**55**	**8**	**-**	**-**	**9**	**2**	**2**	**-**	**-**	**-**	**3**	**-**	**-**	**136**	**30**	**57**

Top Goal Scorer for Hull City three times along with winning the Young Player of the Year and Senior Player of the Year

1991-92	Middlesbrough	8	11	3	1	3	-	-	-	-	-	-	-	-	-	-	9	14	3
Total		**8**	**11**	**3**	**1**	**3**	**-**	**-**	**-**	**-**	**-**	**-**	**-**	**-**	**-**	**-**	**9**	**14**	**3**

1992-93	Glasgow Celtic	19	10	13	1	1	-	3	-	2	1	-	-	-	-	-	24	11	15
1993-94	Glasgow Celtic	1	6	2	-	-	-	-	2	3	-	-	-	-	-	-	1	8	5
Total		**20**	**16**	**15**	**1**	**1**	**-**	**3**	**2**	**5**	**1**	**-**	**-**	**-**	**-**	**-**	**25**	**19**	**20**

Top Goal Scorer for Celtic

1993-94	Barnsley	25	-	12	4	-	1	-	-	-	-	-	-	-	-	-	29	-	13
1994-95	Barnsley	38	5	12	1	-	-	4	-	-	-	-	-	-	-	-	43	5	14
1995-96	Barnsley	37	3	17	1	1	-	3	-	3	-	-	-	-	-	-	41	4	20
Total		**100**	**8**	**41**	**6**	**1**	**1**	**7**	**-**	**3**	**-**	**-**	**-**	**-**	**-**	**-**	**113**	**9**	**47**

Top Goal Scorer for Barnsley twice

1996-97	Huddersfield Town	38	-	17	2	-	-	5	-	2	-	-	-	-	-	-	45	-	19
1997-98	Huddersfield Town	4	1	-	-	-	-	2	-	1	-	-	-	-	-	-	6	1	1
Total		**42**	**1**	**17**	**2**	**-**	**-**	**7**	**-**	**3**	**-**	**-**	**-**	**-**	**-**	**-**	**51**	**1**	**20**

Top Goal Scorer for Huddersfield Town once

1997-98	Burnley	19	-	9	-	-	-	-	-	-	-	-	-	5	-	3	24	-	12
1998-99	Burnley	39	1	19	1	-	2	1	-	1	-	-	-	-	-	-	41	1	22
1999-00	Burnley	39	2	27	4	-	-	1	-	-	-	-	-	1	-	-	45	2	27
2000-01	Burnley	18	22	9	1	1	1	2	2	5	-	-	-	-	-	-	21	25	15
2001-02	Burnley	-	17	4	-	-	-	-	-	-	-	-	-	-	-	-	-	17	4
2001-02	*Blackpool (loan)*	*4*	-	*1*	-	-	-	-	-	-	-	-	-	-	-	-	*4*	-	*1*
2002-03	Burnley	-	1	-	-	1	-	-	-	-	-	-	-	-	-	-	-	2	-
Total		**119**	**43**	**69**	**6**	**2**	**3**	**4**	**2**	**6**	**-**	**-**	**-**	**6**	**-**	**3**	**135**	**47**	**81**
	ALL	**405**	**107**	**200**	**24**	**7**	**4**	**30**	**6**	**19**	**1**	**-**	**-**	**9**	**-**	**3**	**469**	**120**	**226**

Top Goal Scorer for Burnley three times along with winning the Player of the Year twice and golden boot winner